Be That One In A Hundred

**99 Of 100 Aspiring Screenwriters Fail.
But You Can Be That One...**

Other books for screenwriters by Bill Donovan:

Sell Your Screenplay – The Directory of Producers, Agents And Managers Who Will Look At Your Unsolicited Script (2009)

The Best Script Analysts As Rated By Screenwriters (2010, 2013)

Be That One In A Hundred

99 Of 100 Aspiring Screenwriters Fail.
But You Can Be That One...

A guide to avoiding the mistakes many aspiring screenwriters make, as told by producers, agents, readers, and contest judges and managers

By Bill Donovan
Former Editor and Publisher
Of Creative Screenwriting Magazine

Publisher:

Bill Donovan
BeThatOne Publishing
PO Box 6735
Big Bear Lake CA 92315
bill@bethatoneinahundred.com

For permission requests, write to the author at:
William Donovan
PO Box 6735
Big Bear Lake CA 92315
bill@bethatoneinahundred.com

Ordering Information – Quantity sales:

Special discounts are available on quantity purchases by schools, nonprofits, associations, corporations, and others. For details, contact the publisher at the address above. Orders for the print edition by U.S. trade bookstores and wholesalers: If you cannot find this book through your distributor, please contact the author/publisher at the address above.

Library of Congress Control Number: 2017914815

ISBN 978-0-9994452-0-4 (Amazon paperback)

ISBN 978-0-9994452-1-1 (other trade paperback)
ISBN 978-0-9994452-2-8 (.epub)
ISBN 978-0-9994452-3-5 (Kindle .mobi)

Acknowledgments, Credits, Additional Copyrights

The author wishes to make these acknowledgments and offer these credits:

Numerous movie and TV industry people, including producers, agents, directors, an actor, working screenwriters, and aspiring screenwriters, were kind enough to respond to the author's 2015 and 2016 surveys. Many aspiring screenwriters also responded to surveys for this book.

Without their honest answers to my surveys, this book would not have been possible.

Table of Contents

1: Diverging Paths: Succeeding and Failing Are Choices

Author's Note

To succeed as a screenwriter, you need to know what the industry expects of you and its attitudes toward new screenwriters. The goal of this book is to guide aspiring screenwriters toward success in the industry, and to help writers avoid defeating their own quests to become working screenwriters.

In pursuit of that purpose, it contains pointed comments by industry people about aspiring screenwriters they have encountered. I am truly sorry for any pain their or my comments might cause, but forewarned is forearmed.

I'm not a screenwriting guru. What I do well is research, observation, and tabulating and interpreting the results of my research. I researched these questions for this book:

(1) What are aspiring screenwriters doing wrong (in the views of people in the movie and TV industry); and

(2) What can aspiring screenwriters do to avoid these mistakes?

Sources Of The Information In This Book

Most of the information herein came from surveys of hundreds of agents, producers, readers for producers and studios, screenplay consultants, contest managers, contest judges, working screenwriters, directors, and actors, and from a followup survey of aspiring writers. Chapter 15 provides more details on those surveys.

These surveys and interviews reveal that many of them hold very negative views of the errors discussed in this book, and of writers who make them.

In contrast, most of the aspiring screenwriters who responded to my screenwriter survey don't regard the issues raised by industry people as real mistakes, but as acceptable leeway, or as minor imperfections which can be ignored.

That is not to say that every industry person regards every matter discussed here with equal weight. However, every mistake described here is regarded as important by some industry people.

Since you have no control over which readers or producers or contest judges will look at your work, then every "mistake" (in the eyes of the industry) or industry pet peeve, no matter how minor, could be a career-killer.

Who is more right, you as the writer, or them, the industry? It doesn't matter. What does matter is that they make the buying decisions, and that it's a buyer's market.

So they make the rules.

I don't mean to imply that the industry's harsh judgments are "right" in any moral sense or in terms of what is fair. Nor do I mean to imply that they're wrong, in the same sense.

The goal of this book, again, is to report what people in the industry want and expect, and to explain why aspiring screenwriters need to heed what they say in order to succeed.

As a group, aspiring screenwriters are judged by those who stand out. Unfortunately, the bad stands out a lot more vividly than the good. Here's a brief list of the kinds of "mistakes" (by their definition) which they say they see often, and which they dislike, and which you, therefore, need to avoid in order to maximize your chances of success as a screenwriter:

Bad grammar
Bad spelling
Basic formatting mistakes
Basic bad screenwriting
Bad manners
Bad attitudes about receiving criticism
Bad attitudes about rewriting
Big egos.

Let me add one more: weak or nonexistent marketing.

Expecting others to do your selling. See chapter 8.

A Comment From A Struggling, Hard-Working Screenwriter

In my survey of screenwriters, one of my questions was whether respondents had ever submitted a script knowing that it was deficient. A followup question asked, "If so, why?" One aspiring screenwriter gave this response to that second question:

> It was the best result I could reach after trying hard for ten years and ending up so poor that I had to turn the page, leave my noisy rathole and get a proper job at least for a while. Also, it's very hard to know when to stop the obsessive rewriting that will lead you nowhere, because nobody cares about your shit anyway...

To me, this comment captures the very heart of aspiring screenwriters' long and painful journey to ... success for a few, but most of the time, to eventually giving up. It is very difficult to set aside time for writing month after week, year after month, decade after year. One can readily see from this honest statement why a writer would send out work while knowing that its flaws would probably draw the opprobrium of producers, agents, and their readers.

It's tempting to offer the "Well, maybe you should have..." sort of advice to this sufferer of the screenwriting fever. I won't say any such thing. I feel for this writer. I feel for you and your struggle.

"The customer is always right."

Is this old adage really true? When there are at least a hundred vendors of a product in a marketplace for every buyer of their products, then yes, it is true.

That is not to say it is "fair," or that there are no exceptions to it. However, it is true in the sense that in any market which has vastly more vendors than buyers, the buyers have all the bargaining power.

That is the case with the marketplace for screenplays. As a screenwriter, you are one of at least 100,000 vendors of a script or scripts each year. By any rational estimate, there are at most 2,000 purchases of spec screenplays per year. Most of these purchases are made by independent producers, paying amounts well below the Writers Guild of America-West minimums. In addition, writers who are industry insiders account for probably about half the script purchases and options (more on this below). There are credible lower estimates of total script sales, but I could not find any credible higher estimates.

Because of these numbers, producers have almost all the bargaining power. They can dictate not only the terms of the deal with you, but also the very rules of the marketplace.

There are ways in which you can improve your bargaining power. However, there are many more ways to diminish your bargaining power, or to utterly destroy it, for now or even permanently. Most of this book is about those self-sabotaging actions and how to avoid them.

Does this all seem terribly unfair to you? It certainly does seem unfair to many screenwriters, whose complaints are documented in chapters 9-12.

And yes, it is "unfair," in the sense that you have but two choices: abide by the unwritten rules, terms, and conventions of the industry, or quit. As an unproduced screenwriter, you don't have the choice of setting or negotiating separate rules, terms, and conditions for yourself, and there's no likelihood that the rules will change in favor of screenwriters in the foreseeable future.

No One Asked You To Send Them Your Screenplays

However, in a narrow but realistic sense, these unwritten

rules, terms, and conventions of the industry are not unfair at all. That sense is this:

 • No one begged you to write screenplays.

 • No one lured you in with an offer of a purchase or a writing job.

 • No one is asking you to send your spec screenplays to them, except to the extent that responding to your begging for the favor of a read is "asking you."

So the situation is not "unfair" because it was entirely your idea to become one of so many writers hoping to sell your wares to people who didn't invite you to do so.

Yes, I know that this is very difficult to accept. I'm sorry to have to rub your nose in this truth, and in the fact that it's very hard to break in as a screenwriter. However, you are better off if you're prepared.

I read a New Yorker article* about a screenwriter named Kenya Barris, who succeeded in breaking into the business back in the year 2000, using a combination of talent, initiative, acceptance into a fast-track writing program for minorities, and contacts he made. He found work on a few TV shows.

Then, in 2004, he was let go from "Listen Up," a sitcom. So he was out. Done. Career apparently over.

Then, while raising three children, and with his wife in medical school, he wrote 19 pilots – nineteen – before finally breaking back in again as the executive producer (head writer) of "**black**ish," his hit ABC sitcom.

 * The article was written by Emily Nussbaum, the Pulitzer-Prize-winning TV critic for the New Yorker. If you want to write for TV and you don't already read her writing, then I recommend that you do. She is a brilliant analyst of what makes a TV series work.

It's often that difficult. Yet, if you read the "screenwriter complaints" chapters in this book, you'll see that many would-be writers, who have written a script or two, complain with great passion about how unfair the industry is.

Is your journey emotionally brutal? Yes. Will you spend years making a serious effort to be a screenwriter, and even then, not make it? Possibly. Is that unfair? Why? What is unfair about you not receiving something that no one offered or promised you?

***

There is good news in this book. It is that heeding the industry's unwritten rules and terms of doing business will vastly improve your chances. Most of the people you're competing against will either choose to remain ignorant of the industry's unwritten conventions, rules and terms of doing business, or they will choose to ignore them on the grounds that "They don't apply to 'me.'"

Or worst of all, some will complain, in less-than-diplomatic language.

Let them. By self-disqualifying, they improve your relative chances of success.

It's About How To Succeed, Despite The Obstacles

This book seeks to offer the opposite of "Why Most Aspiring Screenwriters Fail..." It is about avoiding those self-defeating actions which foreordain tens of thousands of would-be screenwriters to failure.

It is about how to succeed despite these harsh realities:

1. About Those Numbers: 100,000-plus Scripts, Fewer Than 2000 Sales

Estimates of the number of people writing screenplays worldwide in any given year range as high as a million, according to a 2012 Script Magazine article by Corey Mandell.

Regarding the number of sales, I read one online estimate to the effect that only about 50 spec screenplays are sold per year.

I'm sure that estimate is hogwash. It is low by at least a thousand when one counts both movie and TV scripts sold to the traditional Hollywood outlets, to newer independent producers, to web-based independent shows, and to Web-based major independents like Netflix and Amazon.

With no central reporting agency, no one has an actual hard number. Therefore, for purely illustrative purposes, in this book I use the 100,000 estimate of spec scripts written and 2,000 sold (half of those by insiders). Both are probably in the ballpark, and thus, they are useful as a convenience – but again, they are estimates. No one compiles hard, reliable numbers.

2. The "Insider" Competition:

According to a recently available (2016) WGA-west report, there were 8,704 WGA-west members in 2014. Of those, 4,983 reported that they were working at the time they were surveyed on writing projects. Those numbers fluctuate annually, but not by much.

If about half of all WGA-west writers are already working, then some of that work is in spec script sales. So the number of sales by unproduced, unrepresented writers is much lower than 2,000 sales per year, given that so much of the screenwriting work actually paid for by the industry, including spec scriptwriting, is done by people who have already made it into the Writers Guild.

3. You Have A Bad (Collective) Reputation:

The worst of the harsh realities is that industry professionals as a group, and especially producers and agents, have a low collective opinion of unproduced, uncredited, aspiring screenwriters. The survey data which forms the basis for much of this book not only confirms, but expands on that fact in some detail, and provides many examples and illustrations.

The good news is that you can take yourself out of that collective bad-reputation group, and most of what you need to do so is fairly easy.

Does This Book "Take The Industry's Side"?

No, it quite emphatically does not "take the industry's side." It reports the industry's beliefs, demands, rules, and negative remarks about aspiring screenwriters without much criticism from me. Why have I largely spared the industry from criticism? Because it seems pointless to criticize when all the yakking you or I could do isn't going to change things.

This book takes the side of the aspiring screenwriter who is burning inside to make it in the industry, and who has the talent and temperament for the job of screenwriter as it really is. It takes the side of the screenwriter who can write winning work and employ winning strategies when virtually all the bargaining power is on the side of the buyers of screenplays.

My purpose in telling you what the industry says about aspiring writers is not to discourage, but to help you beat the odds and succeed by avoiding behaviors which lead to failure.

This is not to say you have to like the industry's unwritten rules, conventions, and terms of doing business. Any rational person should feel pain going through rejections, traveling the long and uncertain pathway to maybe someday being paid as a screenwriter, suffering the embarrassment of showing early work that doesn't pass muster, living with the hardship of having to write in one's spare time while holding down a day or night job, having to do unpaid rewrites if your screenplay is sold or optioned to a producer who is not a Writers Guild signatory, and then, even after having been once produced, facing still more rejections.

The industry people speaking up in this book tell you what they expect. With some exceptions,* what they say is unequivocally and abundantly clear. If you can digest it all, and if you can stand these working conditions, then you have a far greater chance of success than most aspiring writers.

* Defining what constitutes a great screenplay, other that listing its characteristics in a general way or offering examples,

is next to impossible. The definition itself differs from producer to producer. Some producers see beauty in a story which touches the heart or sees into the human soul. Others see it as a hefty box office. For most, it's some of both.

Why Many Aspiring Screenwriters Need This Book

A chapter in this book quotes a would-be screenwriter's responses to a survey I did in 2013. His comments got me thinking about how the belief systems and assumptions of aspiring screenwriters can be self-defeating. I started recalling and collecting other anecdotal information on mistakes I'd seen aspiring screenwriters make.

I saw patterns; many hopeful screenwriters seemed to make the same mistakes.

So, this thought came to mind:

Why should you have to spend years failing, when, in one small book, the entertainment industry could tell you what it expects and what you might be doing "wrong" from the points of view of the people you're trying to win over as buyers, employers, and business partners?

To answer that question, I surveyed a large number of producers, agents, readers for studios, producers, and agents, contest executives and judges, screenwriting teachers, and screenplay consultants. I interviewed some. The goal was to determine whether their views on the mistakes made by aspiring screenwriters matched mine.

Their collective views turned out to be much more negative overall than mine.

There Is a Successful Screenwriter "Type"

In the spring of 2007, when I took over Creative Screenwriting Magazine, the Screenwriting Expo, and their related screenplay contests, I began to have occasional contact with writers of box-office leaders and Oscar-winning movies.

That first spring, the Writers' Guild-west invited me to a

media event with screenwriters whose work was being produced in major studio releases that year. They, the successful writers, and we, the entertainment news media, were given the opportunity to mingle in an informal way.

There, I had a discussion with Christopher Markus and Stephen McFeely, the two writing partners who were credited on the three "Chronicles of Narnia" movies.

These two were and are big-time, successful Hollywood writers. Here is what stood out most: How well-mannered, calm, respectful, and polite they were, and that they took quite a bit of time to converse with a complete stranger who had just come into the periphery of the business.

Also, between 2007 and 2010, I had a few in-person and telephone discussions with William Goldman, who, year after year, paid his own way from New York City to California to appear at the Screenwriting Expo for an hour of dialogue and questions and answers from aspiring screenwriters. His kindness to screenwriters, his grace, and his good manners always impressed me.

At the Expo, Goldman always wanted his appearance on stage to be a colloquy with another high-level screenwriter. One year, I approached Aaron Sorkin at our Creative Screenwriting screening of his movie, "Charlie Wilson's War," and asked him to be the other screenwriter in the Goldman colloquy at that year's Expo. He, too, was quite gracious, and in fact, he said he'd be honored. He told me that William Goldman vetted some of his screenplays – an act of mentorship.

Also, I know three produced screenwriters in personal life. Character traits which stands out in these individuals: Their calm. Their perfect manners. In conversation, their intelligence shines through with never a stridently ignorant remark. Two of the three I know well enough to say that they are exceptionally social people and unusually kind human beings; I haven't had enough contact with the third to say whether that is true of him, but I suspect that it is.

I asked one of them about the experience of getting "notes" (criticism) from studio executives and having to rewrite from those notes. I asked because, of all the complaints producers and others in the industry have about would-be screenwriters, the inability to accept a critique is the most common and the most vivid of behavioral issues they see.

This working screenwriter said the experience doesn't terribly bother him, even though notes are sometimes contradictory or irrelevant, and sometimes even juvenile. It's just part of the job.

Then, in August 2017, after I'd finished what I thought was the final version of this book, I ran across an interview with the screenwriter Scotty Mullen in <u>Script Magazine</u> online. Here's what he is quoted saying about how he landed one of his credited screenwriting jobs:

> ...they were working with another writer on a movie called "The Fast and the Fierce." It's like "Speed" on a plane. The writer wasn't taking their notes, so they came to me and said, "Listen, we think that ... you know, could you collaborate with us?" I said of course.

"The writer wasn't taking their notes."

Please keep that sentence in mind as you read chapters 5 and 6, in which producers vent about screenwriters, and chapter 10, in which aspiring screenwriters vent about producers. In fact, it's worth reading that entire interview with Scotty Mullen in <u>Script</u>, looking closely for something there between the lines, unstated but obvious (I've shortened the link using tinyurl.com: https://tinyurl.com/scriptscottymullen

Here's what to look for between the lines: the number of times that Scotty Mullen must have told a producer, "Can do!" and then dropped whatever else he was doing and delivered what the producer needed.

So A Question Arises ...

Have these successful screenwriters adopted grace and good manners and kindness and "Can do!" attitudes because they are successful, or are they successful in part because they are so diplomatic, so gracious, so respectful, so willing to listen to critiques, and so willing to give a producer what she or he wanted?

If you do not yet know the answer to that question, I do hope that this book will help you figure it out.

***

To End This Introduction: The Soul Of This Book, If It Has One...

If there is a soul to this book, then its prayer goes something like this:

You, the aspiring screenwriter with real potential, are forced for now to stand among a sea of petitioners outside the figurative gates of Hollywood, wishing and hoping to win the attention of those producers within.

However, you have the power to stand apart because your work is good, you are diplomatic and persistent, and you can persuade the industry to read your scripts. You are or soon will be in the one percent who will succeed. Or so I believe and hope. That is my prayer, and the soul of this book.

2: Bugs And Gremlins In The Screenplay

Worst And Most Common Content Mistakes
(As Seen By The Industry)
Spelling, Grammar, And Basic Formatting Errors

In the eyes of many people in the movie and TV industry, spelling and grammar errors are the worst and most self-destructive mistakes the writer can make within the screenplay, followed closely by incorrect formatting.

The survey results showed, unequivocally, that these are the mistakes complained about most, by far.

However, not every producer feels that way. One producer wrote to me recently:

> Producer here, just a moment of reality for you brother: I don't care if spelling is off, couldn't give a bannana if formatting is off. Is the story compelling? All that matters.

His point of view is valid – for him. (And this is just a bit unkind, but he illustrates his point by misspelling "banana.")

However, many others said in survey responses that they find corrupt grammar, creative spelling, and incorrect formatting to be distracting at best, and a personal insult at worst. See some examples below.

Even more than producers, their script readers tend to be strict on grammar. And that is as it should be. Here's why:

It is difficult to read someone else's screenplay and visualize the characters and the action, and to try to grasp the characters' goals and desires, and at the same time, to visualize the imaginary world the writer has tried to create. When the spelling, grammar, and basic formatting of a screenplay are not correct, the producer or agent (or, more likely, his or her reader) can easily lose focus on important facts of the story.

As focus fades, interest fades. By the third or fourth grammatical, spelling, or formatting error in the first few pages, with a stack of other screenplays in the queue behind yours, you and your screenplay are probably toast.

Here's another fact of life: good grammar and structure tend to correlate with good storytelling. In my experience – and I've been editing other people's work for 48 years now, including more than a hundred screenplays, and I've read another hundred or so as a contest judge – it is rare that someone who can't string sentences together can write that "compelling story" mentioned above. The skills of language and storytelling tend to go together.

If you're already a professional writer from another field, trying to write your first, or fifth, or whatever screenplay, you're probably thinking, "Well, of course!" As a pro, you're probably thinking that spelling, grammar, and basic formatting mistakes are uncommon, right?

Surprise. They are not.

If you're new to screenwriting, you might also be thinking, "They have people to fix that sort of thing, so small details like these shouldn't matter." In fact, some respondents to the writer survey for this book said exactly that, in their own words.

Surprise again: You are the "They have people" person. And these things matter a lot.

Along with being the worst mistakes in the eyes of many industry people, spelling, grammar, and basic formatting mistakes are also the most common mistakes they see. Read this sampling of their comments:

Worst Mistakes:

Spelling and/or grammatical errors. If you can't be bothered to proofread your script properly, why should I (or anyone else) be bothered to read it? Also, if you can't spell or understand grammar, then perhaps writing isn't for you. – *Hollywood Production Executive*

Not proofreading ... a manuscript full of typos will end up in the trash. It's difficult to recognize a good story hidden underneath a bunch of typos and misspelled words. – *Producer*

It's CRITICAL that all work be proofread several times as mistakes are often missed. – *Screenplay contest judge*

Too many of the scripts I read are poorly formatted and seem to have been submitted to me with minimal proofreading. Without making these simple fixes, I have a hard time really looking at the actual content. – *Producer*

1. Spelling mistakes. 2. Poor Grammar. – *Producer/Production Exec; also a Screenwriting Consultant/Script Analyst*

1. Excessive typos & spelling errors. 2. Sloppy *formatting. – Producer/ Production Exec; Actor; Writer*

Bad grammar and spelling errors –*Producer/Production Exec*

Most Common Mistakes:

Grammar mistakes – *Producer/ Production Exec; also a Screenwriting Consultant or Script Analyst*

1. Incorrect format. 2. Spelling & typos. – *Producer/Production Exec*

1. Improper format. 2. Typos and incorrect grammar. This includes lack of proper punctuation, such as not using commas when needed. – *Producer/Production Exec*

Attention to detail – or the lack thereof – from simple grammar (because they don't bother re-reading the screenplays), to the more intricate stuff of structure, character, etc. – *Producer/Production Exec*

Spelling and grammatical issues. –
Producer/Production Exec

And so on. There were many more comments like these.

The industry people above, and others who responded to the survey, are clearly hoping to pass on this message:

If you represent yourself to be a screenwriter, then you have to be a professional writer, in every sense of the word "professional." Most of all, you must have a professional writer's command of the English language.

If you don't, you might sell one screenplay by hiring a professional copy editor and proofreader to help you polish it. However, in the long run, you will need to learn from your copy editor because otherwise, your inability to manage basic formatting, grammar, and spelling will eventually be exposed.

These comments, from an aspiring writer and an agent, were both illustrative and, juxtaposed against one another, illuminating:

The Aspiring Writer:

> Some people may have great ideas, but their writing level may not be quite as polished yet, but if the producers could still work with you and negotiate something, then it creates a win-win situation. – ***Screenwriter response to the screenwriter survey***

The Agent:

> I get writers all the time who say, "Don't worry about the format, they have people to fix that..." I tell them you are those people, so if you are wrong, how will a producer ever be able to feel confident that you can not only write but rewrite? – ***Agent who has also been a Screenwriting Teacher, in Contest Executive Management, and a***

Filmmaker

"But ... but ... but ... " you say. "That agent is being unfair...That writer is right."

May I suggest that you give some thought to dropping that line of thinking?

It's life, not the entertainment industry, which is "unfair" in the sense you mean. Some people are endowed with command of language; others are not. Some people are endowed with the doggedness to work at a thing until they get it right; others settle for an early draft or a halfway job.

That is not to say you should quit trying to write screenplays if your basic writing skills and your command of screenplay structure and format aren't yet up to professional standards.

It means only that you need to work on your writing or get editing and proofreading help before you show your work.

I proofread and make notes on screenplays. One fact I have noticed about my proofreading clients is that most are good to very good writers, but that some of them were making the same few mistakes again and again. Some, after seeing their mistakes corrected in proofreading, stopped making those mistakes. Studying what a proofreader does with your draft is a relatively quick and relatively inexpensive writing course.

The industry is pleading with you to learn and polish your work before submitting it. Again, you are the "they have people" people.

A Few Words On Rewriting

Experienced professional writers know that "writing is rewriting."

However, when discussing writing with relative newcomers (people who haven't been making money as professional writers), I sometimes get the impression that this

17

phrase doesn't really sink in. Perhaps this anecdote may help:

I've been working on another piece of writing, a two-volume book, for about a decade.

I've written the opening of the second volume from scratch at least six times, maybe eight times. I've fiddled with that opening numerous other times. I don't mean a few paragraphs. Currently, that opening is 40-plus pages. It has been as long as 48 pages. That's 40 or more pages, completely re-conceived and redone, six to eight times.

However, it still doesn't seem right. My instincts tell me that it should be 10 to 15 fast-moving pages, not 40-plus. So I will go back and try again.

Why didn't I outline first, you ask? Well, I did. Multiple times. The outline kept changing, too. It happens.

Does this mean I'm not a good writer? I think not. Over the past 51 years, I've been paid to write daily news, magazine articles, speeches, laws, (yes, laws), U.S. Senate committee reports on laws, reference books on screenwriting and information technology, computer manuals, and hundreds of advertising pieces that persuaded people to send money. I have five national business journalism awards and three cash awards for contest-winning screenplays. Given that experience, I don't think incompetence on my part is the problem.

It's just that every now and then, it takes six to eight or more rewrites from scratch, over a period of months or more, to figure out what a passage or a whole work should say. Usually, this isn't the case, but it happens.

Writing is rewriting. And sometimes, it's rewriting times six or eight. I have the impression, from the comments of screenwriters in later chapters, that some new screenwriters don't understand how much rewriting goes into creating an acceptably good screenplay.

3: More (And More Complex) Mistakes

These May Send A Screenplay
Straight To The 'Reject' File

Industry people in my survey identified other kinds of content mistakes, beyond spelling, grammar, and basic formatting, which they say are either common or among the worst (again, in their eyes), and which can cause a screenplay and its author to be rejected. Before sending work out to the industry or to contests, be sure it doesn't have any of the issues on this checklist:

✔ Cheating On White Space to Make A Screenplay Look Shorter

> Most (screenplays) are too long, but disguised to be shorter than they are by cheating the layout or using big blocks of text. Poor white space. If done properly, most would be five or more pages longer than presented. *-- Consultant/Script Analyst, Screenplay Contest Management*

Many white-space issues, as most screenwriters know, are solved quite easily by using the templates in your screenwriting software – Final Draft or Movie Magic Screenwriter or one of the online systems, such as Celtx or WriterDuet.

A template forces you to use the correct margins and spacing between elements, leaving fewer ways to cram a screenplay into fewer pages than it should actually occupy.

However, the software doesn't correct every kind of cramming. A common form of cramming is putting action description into fat blocks to make the screenplay take up fewer pages. This is the easiest cheat for a producer, agent, reader, or contest judge to see.

Advice: don't do it. The industry likes white space. One way to create that white space is to give each action or single set of actions by one character its own paragraph.

Separating actions into their own paragraphs gives the writer another benefit. You know that you're not supposed to dictate shots to the director (unless it's unavoidable). However, giving each camera setup its own paragraph is a way to suggest shots, giving you a greater role in the creative process.

So if an action is complex enough to require its own camera angles, put it into a separate paragraph, with white space above and below. That white space is a secret weapon which skilled screenwriters know. It is a way to signal to the director that a new camera setup is needed without actually saying so.

✔ Too Much Description; Too Much Exposition; Over-Written Dialogue.

A common error is length and too much exposition and novelistic writing. Again, this is writing without studying the art form. -- *Screenplay Contest Judge, Contest Executive Management*

Too many directorial descriptions. – *Producer/Production Executive*

Excessive description – *Producer/Production Executive*

I read a lot of scripts where the dialogue is repetitive, over-explained, and too technical and teachy. – *Producer/Production Executive*

The phrase, "writing without studying the art form," can refer to a multitude of sins. One of the worst sins is description which states facts or thoughts which cannot be seen or heard. See the commentary below on "Failing To Write Visually." Another sin is that painful sort of dialogue which is written purely to tell the plot to the audience.

How much description is too much?

This is the difficult part, because as a writer, you see it the way you see it, and it's hard to step out of your visualization. Moreover, you want your story to retain its uniqueness. Some producers, readers, and contest judges suggest a guideline such as this:

Any descriptive details not needed in the story, such as a physical description of a character, place, or thing, when that physical description does not play a role in the story, can probably be cut.

✔ Too Short; Too Little Description

> Pacing and flow are super important. I find some writers will write too choppy and aren't exploiting the scenario through the dialogue and in the layers of the action. **-- Producer, Production Exec or Management**

In my screenplay proofreading business, I see as much under-writing as excessively long descriptions. I wonder whether some writers get the word that description should not be excessive, and then go overboard in the opposite direction, writing so tersely as to provide an insufficient visual picture of the place and people.

For example, one client's screenplay opens with a scene something like this:

```
INT. JENNY'S OFFICE - DAY

Bare office. Desks at opposite sides of
the room.

JENNY SMITH, a young, confident
heartbreaker, types away at her computer.
She pauses to read her work.
```

I made some changes to avoid using my client's exact

words, but this was the basically the entire first scene. Consider the facts that this is the <u>opening scene</u> of the screenplay and that Jenny and her office mate have entirely different personalities, career goals, and work habits (which would be reflected by what is on their desks and in their personal spaces). The writer could and should have given us a few visual cues about them, and also about the business.

For example, there could be visuals such as posters of magazine ads on the wall, chosen for the kind of ads the agency produces. There could be a couple of small, telling details about the furniture to hint at both how the business is doing financially, and whether its style is trendy or staid.

Also, except for the "young" part of the description of Jenny, which the writer could have said more clearly by stating her age or approximate age, it's a completely internal, non-visual description. What is the director supposed to aim the camera at, in the way of physical details or actions, to show us "confident" or whatever the writer really means by "heartbreaker"?

Also, what does she gather around herself? Pictures of family on the desk? No pictures of family, which might hint at no family or estrangement from family? What about her handbag? Hermes or Prada, or inexpensive and utilitarian?

And is she a workaholic who eats at her desk (food remnants, coffee stains, et cetera)? Is her wastebasket or email inbox overflowing with anything? Is her desk or computer busy with client work, or not? Et cetera. And how do these visual details differ from those of her office-mate? The writer could have briefly described her clothes, makeup, nails, footwear, and purse, and contrasted them with those of her office-mate.

We definitely don't need <u>all</u> of these suggested details in this scene, or even most of them....Just enough to start us on what happens next. Instead, the writer doesn't visually describe either Jenny or the office at all. Why? My impression is that these details are missing because he doesn't really know who Jenny is.

Again, this is the <u>opening</u> scene, in which we need to know a bit more. We need to have the theme and milieu set for the rest of the movie. Writing which is this spare signals to a producer or agent or contest judge that the writer might lack the skill to reveal with visuals, or might have chosen not to try.

Here is another "person sitting in an office" example, changed just a bit from the way it was written by another client. This is the first meeting in the story between the protagonist and his boss. Like the scene above, it's static and empty of details:

```
INT. ADMINISTRATOR JONES'S OFFICE - DAY

ADMINISTRATOR JONES, about 65, heavy, is
sitting at his desk. There is a KNOCK on
the door.
```

I suggested something like the following to my client as an off-the-top-of-my-head example of how this scene could be juiced up in a way that tells us much more. This is intentionally a bit over-done for effect:

```
INT. ADMINISTRATOR JONES'S OFFICE - DAY

ADMINISTRATOR JONES is about 65. The
second of his double chins descends his
neck in a wattle, a paunch hides his belt,
and his hindquarters spread to the very
edges of his leather executive chair. He
clips his fingernails and glides the
clippings into a neat little pile on an
otherwise empty, highly polished teak
desktop.

There's a sharp, rapid-fire KNOCK on the
door. Jones quickly gathers the clippings
and drops them into a matching teak
wastebasket, its plastic lining immaculate
and otherwise empty.

He frowns briefly at the door, then pulls
several colored hanging file folders at
```

```
random from his filing drawer, spreads
them out on the desktop, and pulls his
expensive-brand silver-plated pen from his
suit jacket pocket. Only then does he
clear his throat, in that way some bosses
have of preparing to hand down a
pronouncement from on high.
```

Again, I have over-described a bit for the sake of example.

Yes, Jones still "is sitting" at his desk, but this description doesn't say it in so many words. It doesn't have to. It is intentionally full of, even overloaded with, the sort of details which tell us or hint that Jones has grown old and overweight in a job, that he likes the trappings of his position (teak, leather, silver-plating), that he has nothing of substance to do, that he's quite adept at and content with doing nothing but grooming himself, and that he feels a need to hide these facts about himself from the aggressive door-knocking person who is about to enter.

The fact that he has a fingernail clipper in his office is a small, telling detail in and of itself. The fact that grooming his fingernails matters to him, while he has let himself grow obese, suggests a certain inability to see himself as he is seen by others.

Giving Jones this moment allows us to infer that he doesn't want the boat rocked, that the person knocking aggressively is a boat-rocker; and that, if possible, Jones is going to find a way to say, "No."

On the other hand, if every scene opening were long like this, it would be far too much. My description above certainly leans in the direction of far too much, but it does introduce an important character, who is a passive but powerful roadblock to the protagonist's pursuit of his or her goal, and it does so in a very visual manner. The fact of Jones's importance in the story lends merit to taking time, just once, to give some telling details about him.

✔ Failing to Write Visually: Ignoring the "Show, Don't Say" Rule.

It's not merely an ironclad rule in screenwriting that you have to tell the story visually and aurally. It is screenwriting itself. Not a word should appear on the page which the camera cannot see or the sound equipment can't pick up. This is often stated as the "Show, don't say" rule.

Yes, this rule is often ignored in screenplays written by experienced, produced screenwriters. However, following their example makes a new writer look like an amateur who doesn't know how to write a screenplay. Produced writers have made their bones in the industry and can get away with a few dents and bends to the rules. A new writer should always adhere to "Show, don't say."

Seize every opportunity to tell the story in visuals and sounds. "Show, don't say" may seem like a difficult constraint to the beginning screenwriter. It is certainly difficult for the uncreative. However, it is a huge advantage for the skilled aspiring writer who wants to stand out. It forces you to find creative visual and sound elements to tell the story. A screenplay reader for a producer will spot good visual storytelling right away – and will spot its opposite even faster.

However, do be brief about it, choosing only the telling, needed visual and aural details.

✔ Mashing Genres Together

> While this can work, it's not a good idea to start out as a screenwriter like this - going from comedy to drama or thriller for example half way through... *-- **Producer, Production Exec or Management***

Mashing genres together creates two challenges. The first is successfully pulling it off. The second, equally or more difficult, is finding a market for it. A producer who works in comedy seeks comedies; a producer who works in the horror market, with a completely different demographic of viewers, seeks horror scripts. The set of producers who are seeking horror-comedy is not the sum of the two; it is a much smaller subset, which excludes most of both groups of producers. So as a new writer, you create a marketing hurdle for yourself when you write a genre-mixing screenplay. You are trying to persuade people who know their audiences to try something different on those audiences.

If a genre-crossing screenplay of yours is really good, then ignore this rule. On the other hand, if you think it's really good, and no one buys it...Well, I hate to say, "I told you so," but I told you so.

✔ Bad Structure; Failing To Outline Carefully; Failing To Do Rewrites

Three-act isn't necessary, but many writers don't spend enough time in the outline phase. – *Producer, Production Exec or Management*

Many screenplays are episodic, without any clear forethought about where they are going, often just written off the top of the writers' heads. Then, when given notes to improve, many do a surface re-write without addressing issues, and many don't enter again and don't bother to re-write -- which is unfortunate, as re-writing is the key to screenwriting. **-- *Screenplay Contest Judge, Contest Executive Management***

Hasn't done enough drafts - script not ready. **-- *Producer, Production Exec or Management and Screenplay Consultant***

I think that a weak second act that is also too long, where the story simply drags on and on without a clear rising sense of action, is quite common, as are deus-ex-machina endings or illogical plot points that are merely there for the author's convenience, but create a break in the suspension of disbelief. Another is writing that is simply over the top, overly dramatic, not believable or human in any way. *-- **Screenplay Contest Judge, Contest Executive Manager***

In fairness to aspiring writers, nearly all of us have great difficulty seeing what is wrong with our own work.

A few years ago, a contest-winning screenwriter, a longtime friend of mine, asked me to critique his screenplay. I was quite flattered, because...Well, because who was I to critique his work? He'd been a working film editor in Hollywood for years before turning to screenwriting, and he had already taken many classes and rewritten and polished the screenplay as far as he could. Me? I was just the guy who had bought a magazine in the business (and had written three spec screenplays which had gone nowhere 20 years earlier). One of my comments was that the action was driving the protagonist, rather than the protagonist driving the action. (My other comments were very likely useless.)

To my surprise, he thanked me and rewrote details of core early scenes to put the protagonist in charge of his own decisions and actions. (Very likely, other people he asked to comment had made the same observation in their own ways, so I doubt that I deserved all the credit for that observation.) I was quite surprised that he thought I had nailed a key point. I was doubly surprised that he had not been able to see it himself until it was said. The screenplay later won a significant contest prize and was purchased by a producer.

I still think there was nothing brilliant about my comment. However, sometimes, even a very good writer can't see what he or she can't see until someone points it out. That is an essential part of the process.

Yet, judging by the comments of producers in later chapters, many would-be screenwriters refuse to solicit such information, and when it is offered, respond with horrid manners. In contrast, my friend thanked me for saying what I thought was wrong with his screenplay.

Horrid manners, in fact, are the subject of the next chapter.

✔ Bad Formatting

I'd say that overall formatting is a huge issue. Many (aspiring screenwriters) don't bother to even Google the basics. **-- *Screenplay Contest Judge, Contest Executive Management.***

Form is content for me, so bad format, or what translates to a misunderstanding of visual communication, is the worst. **-- *Agent, Screenwriting Teacher, Contest Executive Management, Filmmaker***

In common usage, there is some overlap between the terms "format" and "structure." So it is not completely clear to me whether these two commenters are referring only to that which is strictly format, or whether they also mean whether a screenplay adheres to sound storytelling structure. Be safe: count both as vital elements of a good screenplay.

✔ Failing To Use Screenwriting Software

One producer/production executive cited this as the second-worst problem he sees in the content of spec screenplays

Typing in WORD and not formatting with Final Draft or similar software. **– *Producer, Production* Exec or Management**

The producer didn't say it's a common problem. I've seen it myself in screenplays sent to me by a couple of writers who wanted me to proofread them. I declined both, for two reasons.

One is practical: if, in proofreading, I have to do a fix which makes the line longer, it can throw the formatting of that line or paragraph out of whack. Then, someone has to put that entire paragraph back into the correct margins. This can require a painful number of keystrokes. Well, reformatting is not my job; that's why screenwriting software exists.

The second reason is that failing to use even free online screenwriting software is a clear signal that the writer is not merely an amateur, but probably a brand-new amateur who hasn't taken his or her first screenwriting course.

In one case, the formatting was so awful that I advised the writer to start over -- not only with screenwriting software, but also with basic screenwriting classes. He knew nothing about correct basic formatting, and had cluelessly tried to imitate a screenplay without even the most fundamental understanding.

Yes, it is indeed possible to write a properly-formatted screenplay without screenwriting software. But don't. Even if you know all the indents, you'll waste a lot of time. Also, if you can't afford Final Draft or Movie Magic Screenwriter, there are free and cheap online programs. Celtx.com, Plotbot.com, and Rawscripts.com are free, WriterDuet is free and the Pro edition just $7.99 a month, and Scriptbuddy.com is just $15.50 for three months. Or, if you use a Mac, there's a program called Slugline for $39.95.

Fourth, and most important, people in the industry want to work only with professionals (or with newcomers who know enough to look like one at all times). So if anyone in the industry becomes interested in your work and then finds out that you aren't using screenwriting software, your relationship with that industry person could be over. You must always look and act like a professional. Especially if you're a newbie.

So why would you do all that extra work, make rewriting much more tedious, and sabotage yourself by attempting to write a screenplay in MS Word or some other word processing program?

✔ Is The Premise Movie-Worthy, TV-Worthy, Or Not Worthy?

One of the most common and worst mistakes, according to screenplay readers and some executives, is a premise which is just not a good one for a movie or TV show. Even after readers filter out the majority of scripts, many producers say they see screenplays which (in their eyes) range from dull to awful.

However, how do you tell as you start to write, while immersed in the writing, or even when you think you're finished, that the original idea was good or bad?

This is the most difficult question you face because there is no simple answer.

Given the limits of the survey questions, none of our respondents went into great detail about what constitutes a great subject. You should be able to get some sense of what they do like by reading between the lines of, or extrapolating from, their comments on what they don't like.

However, here are some clues to a bad screenplay:

1. It has a flashback in the first few pages.

2. A large ensemble of characters is introduced in the first 10 pages.

3. The absence of a single, central protagonist-antagonist story line. If your story has an ensemble of characters, but there is no predominant story of a hero/heroine on a quest (or of a flawed character seeking to atone), with an adversary who might make that difficult, you could be writing a piece which won't sell. There are exceptions, of course. The romance, bromance, and buddy comedy genres are usually about two lead stories which intertwine. But again, one usually leads, and it's difficult to write both stories with precisely equal balance between their two storylines.

4. Stories which are purely about sex. Every now and

then, one gets made. It does terribly at the box office, and no one tries to put another into wide release for a couple of years. They don't sell.

5. Exposé journalism about an injustice. Unless there's a central story about individuals, it probably won't translate to a scripted fiction format. Even in a documentary, someone has to be there to push the narrative along.

6. Your intensely-felt story about yourself. The "my teenage years" story is not likely to interest anyone else unless your teenage years were extraordinary, or you have an extraordinarily acute comic eye for your own history.

Here are three online sources with good clues as to subject matter that works and does not work:
https://litreactor.com/columns/10-reasons-your-screenplay-sucks-and-how-to-fix-it
https://www.writersstore.com/10-story-techniques-you-must-use-to-sell-your-script/
http://www.scriptmag.com/features/meet-the-reader-12-signs-of-promising-spec-script

✔ Not Original; Trying to Feed The Audience An Old Meal, Ready To Eat:

Lack of anything original to say in the theme. — *Producer, Production Exec or Management*

Too often, it seems writers write what they think the audience wants instead of writing what they have a unique perspective on. Jill Soloway wrote about something she had a personal connection to, and that is how she made her name. She had a unique perspective. You wouldn't have know that an audience would react to that story, but she personalized it, and that's the difference. — *Producer, Production Exec or Management*

31

Yes, very true. However, in my opinion, Soloway's success isn't due only to the personal connection to the material. She also writes fearlessly and unusually boldly about contemporary life, especially contemporary sexual life, in the way of certain new female comedy voices who have risen very recently. According to a Wikipedia article, Alan Ball, whose work shows cutting-edge sensibilities, hired her for "Six Feet Under" after reading a short story she wrote, called "Courteney Cox's Asshole."

In case you're interested and not too squeamish, that short story could be found, as of this writing, at this URL: http://www.corpse.org/archives/issue_10/ficciones/soloway.htm

Few writers could have written that story. It's both too raw and vulgar, and at the same time, an insightful and funny satire. So, in my view, the sources of Jill Soloway's success are that she writes exactly what today's young, urban-ish female audiences want and that she writes so boldly about subjects covered many times before.

Consider another example, the documentary-style show, "River Monsters."

No, it's not real documentary. It's facts and myths carefully arranged into a very fiction-like narrative. Virtually every episode has the same plot, telling the same "big fish that got away and then didn't" story, week after week. Heroic Jeremy Wade travels to some remote part of the globe where some creature chewed up or ate a native who ventured into the river. Jeremy spends most of the show, between commercial breaks which seem like they're each about half an hour long, riding in a boat or at the river's edge, casting and catching the wrong fish. However, his audience doesn't flip channels because there is always a payoff in the last two minutes: he lands the real-life toothy river monster. It's usually a fish so big it could chew the bumper off a Hummer.

He gets away with the monotony and the interminable commercial interruptions because he delivers the anticipated surprise, the image of the big fish, at the end.

32

So ... Certainly, it's better if a story is original and compelling from the start. But if your story has enough real surprises or insights, you can write in a form and on a theme which otherwise seems worn out. Just be sure to deliver that big fish at the end.

✔ Ignorance of The Filmmaking Process And The Fact That It's A Business.

> They lack knowledge of the filmmaking process. They are not filmmakers and therefore have limited understanding ... – *Producer, Production Exec or Management*

> The most common mistake that I run into is the lack of business sense that the writer has. The majority of writers do not understand that this is a business and the overall script must reflect that. You should not be writing as if your submitting to the local paper or magazine. – *Producer, Production Exec or Management*

Here's a small instance of ignorance of the business end of things:

A screenplay I read and analyzed recently opened with two scenes of two men driving a big truck through a residential neighborhood. The first scene is the two men in the truck. One jumps out. In the second scene, the man who exited the truck approaches a house, hears music, pauses to listen, and his facial expression shows that he's impressed.

That's it. Not only does he never enter the house, but neither of them ever appears again in the script. The next scene, in the house with that musician playing, is the actual start of the movie.

So, in other words, the resources to shoot these two scenes include a big truck, two actors, a crew, maybe half a million dollars' worth of moviemaking equipment, a security team for sidewalk and street traffic control, a caterer, city permits, insurance, probably at least half a day of shooting plus travel time, and then time in the foley and sound-effects rooms in post-production because wild (ambient outdoor) sound usually has to be replaced. In addition, payoffs to neighbors might be needed to keep them from intentionally walking into a shot to ruin it (yes, this happens all the time).

All that and more goes into the budget. And the purpose of all this expense?

To show us that one of the trucking guys is impressed by the music coming from the garage – implying that we, too, should be impressed.

I suggested to the writer that the two scenes be cut. Having the musician play something and impress us, which was already the next scene, is the real opening.

A professional screenwriter already knows this sort of thing. Don't add actors and scenes, especially costly exterior scenes, unless they have a role in the story. Producers expect you to know that, too.

Here's another: Your script has multiple scenes in which characters are sitting in taxicabs moving along city streets in daytime, texting other people and then reading their texts. Important lines of the movie are being texted back and forth.

What's wrong with the above? Well, first, budget. A taxicab moving through a city is an expensive and difficult place to shoot a scene. Moving along a city street, the light changes as you pass through the shadows of tall buildings and the reflections off windows. These light changes make it difficult (or impossible) to match reverse-angle shots or wider shots and closeups. It's darker inside the taxi, so the interior lighting has to balance off the exterior light – which, again, changes as one goes into and emerges from the shadows of tall buildings, and as the sun changes position in the sky. You probably have to do more than one take for timing, and then, you have to move the camera to the other side of the taxi to get reverse angles, and hope that the light matches in the two opposite angles. The same problems arise with the sound.

Then, there are the costs of renting the taxi, permits to shoot on streets, control of traffic, the special camera mounts, other extra equipment, and the expense of feeding a crew on location.

Equally important is this question: Why? Sitting someone in a taxi to thumb and read texts makes for one of the dullest and most static possible ways to shoot a conversation. Why not just have the two people meet? If you must have them text rather than speak, put them both in places more interesting and less costly to shoot in than a taxi, and cut back and forth between them.

✔ Other "Worst" Content Problems Cited By Industry Respondents

A screenplay reader for producers /agents/studios sees these as the <u>most common</u> mistakes seen in spec screenplays from aspiring writers:

1. Story lines that don't track.

2. Stereotypical/cliched characters and plots.

3. Lack of theme.

4. Trying too hard with symbolism.

The <u>worst</u> mistakes, according to this same reader:

1. Characters who are not true to their natures that the writer established, so their choices don't make sense or are surprising, but in a bad way. 2. Also, creating plot points that are not believable in the world the writer created.

"This excludes the obvious poor formatting and spelling errors," the reader adds.

Industry "War Stories" And Recommendations About Screenplay Content:

One of the questions I asked participants in the industry survey was:

Do you have an anecdote or "war story" to share about a particular screenplay illustrating any of the most common or worst mistakes in the content? Or do you have recommendations for screenwriters on the content? If so, please share here.

Here are some responses:

Too many war stories to enumerate. What is fascinating, though, is the number of young screenwriters who believe their particular work is absolutely the best premise since sliced bread. *-- Producer, Production Exec or Management*

Aspiring screenwriters should stick to writing about a subject they are deeply immersed in and fascinated by personally. Do not write a screenplay about something you think the audience will want to read based on market findings of successful movies. It will just come off as dull. Unique and interesting screenplays have strong premise, strong characters and strong dialogue. You can't get a screenplay made into a movie if you don't have compelling characters that will attract cast. **-- Agent**

Insistence that if a company didn't 'get it,' they just didn't read closely enough. Or insistence that certain "plants" in dialogue explain alleged plot twists that (while never shown on the page) are supposed to make the whole script make sense if only the reader/company was smart enough to understand. *-- Producer, Production Exec or Management*

Some writers write to 'shock' or to just get a lot of 'ugly' on the page without really thinking about any kind of clear story with a strong beginning, middle, and end. Some send in very pornographic or sexual pieces, but none of the characters are even likable or relatable whatsoever. There are some years where there is a plethora of pieces with gratuitous nudity, rape, child sexual abuse, etc., as if the writers are not thinking about the end result of really selling their work, rather just getting something off their chests in a really ugly way instead of telling a compelling story about the above subjects. *-- Screenplay Contest Judge, Contest Executive Management*

I would recommend attending speaker panels with credited writers in film and TV. Take courses with small classes/sessions with a screenwriter. Take notes from other writers and read their scripts. Study different writing styles of credited writers in each genre. *-- Producer, Production Exec or Management*

It seems every story I get from non-English-speaking Euro countries (Finland, Romania, Hungary, Sweden, etc.) are thrillers about iconic American characters (FBI, military, political, etc.) in [what they think are] iconically American situations. Yet, the entire premise is built on something very non-American. One Romanian writer sent me two scripts. The first was well written, basically a fantasy romance with the lead character being a 'super-famous Hollywood star,' [the commenter names an actor from a 2005-2009 TV show]. The show had obviously had just hit Romanian TV (a couple years after going off the air in the US), and the perception was that he's a huge star here. The other script was all about an orphan in modern America who grows up in a 3rd-rate orphanage and later establishes a chain of shiny, happy orphanages that offer good healthcare and stop institutional abuses. Not exactly timely. *-- Consultant or Script Analyst, Screenplay Contest Management*

Get in the mind set that this is a business. You are asking someone to risk X amount of dollars to invest in a new writer's idea. It should not be considered a hobby. *-- Producer, Production Exec or Management*

Notice the apparent conflict between the second and sixth comments. One says, in effect, to write what you know, regardless of whether you think it's marketable. The other says just as clearly that if it's not a currently marketable story, it's going nowhere.

Who is right? Unfortunately for you, they both are. In order to sell, a story has to be written from knowledge <u>and</u> it must be currently marketable. It also must have with great emotional appeal. To the extent that you want to model a story on a currently popular movie, it's the heart and emotional appeal you need to take from that movie to yours.

4: You Sent It Out, Knowing It Had Problems

Are Writers Really "Lazy," Or Is There A Deeper Lesson Here?

To be honest, reading non-professional scripts (and even a lot of professional ones) is often an extremely painful process. Boredom seeps in and it's so hard to keep reading through all of the pages ... [among other shortcomings, I see] laziness, lack of attention to detail. — *A director who is also a film/video editor and writer*

Another survey respondent, a producer or production company executive, similarly says that the most common mistake he/she sees is, "Laziness. Not writing constantly." This executive also wrote that the very worst mistake is "Fishing for representation without great work."

What? Lazy? You slaved, without pay, and with slender but deeply-felt hope, over 110 or so pages of creation starting from a blank page (or about 30 or 60 for a teleplay). And then, they have the gall to call you "lazy!"

Yes. That which they call "laziness" is one of the most common complaints the industry makes about aspiring screenwriters. It's a nasty accusation. But is it truly laziness?

In my opinion, no. Industry people who use this term are identifying real problems, but they are using the wrong descriptive word.

In some cases, that which is labeled as "laziness" is incompetence. People who can't spell or put together a grammatically correct sentence, who don't know "it's" from "its," or "their" from "there" or "they're" or who don't use screenplay software, or fail to learn screenplay formatting, or who know nothing of story structure, shouldn't be sending out screenplays until they do. Or never if they can't learn. You can't become a brain surgeon or a truck driver if you can't operate the equipment. What makes some people think they can be professional writers without learning to write?

However, reading through screenwriters' responses in the survey of screenwriters for this book, two other explanations for the "laziness" label stand out. Both are learning opportunities for aspiring writers.

Not "Lazy" At All. "Unaware" Is More Like It

Many new screenwriters are simply unaware of the industry's very high expectations. Industry executives want to deal only with screenwriters who meet professional standards in both the work and behavior. Most producers and agents expect your writing to be grammatically perfect or nearly so, well structured, well researched, and formatted correctly. Anything less is likely to be labeled "lazy." As mentioned above, some aspiring writers mistakenly believe that "they have people" to do the "writing" part of screenwriting. Once again, they don't; you are the "they have people" people.

In addition, they are all looking for that elusive thing, creative uniqueness. Producers want to see stories they haven't seen before. How do they, and how can you, know that your story has that quality? There is no single way or process to tell, except maybe this one: you deliver a story with that essence, and someone buys it. A work may look "lazy" to a producer simply because it's so much like other works she or he has seen.

Another Reason Aspiring Screenwriters Get Stuck With The "Lazy" Label

The survey responses of screenwriters themselves, discussed in chapters 9-12, reveal a second reason for the "lazy" label. Many aspiring screenwriters feel a wholly unrealistic sense of entitlement.

Let me restate a point made above: This is not a matter of what is "fair" or "unfair."

This is about when your feeling of entitlement butts heads with where the power lies. Many screenwriters strongly believe that the industry should change its culture and accommodate to them in many different ways. Many said so quite passionately in their responses to the survey of screenwriters discussed in chapters 9-12.

Bad news: That is not going to happen. The industry's unwritten rules are only slightly more negotiable than the value of Pi or the physical laws of the Universe. Many aspiring writers already understand this. If you are one of those who do, you're probably wondering why I'm saying the obvious.

I'm saying it because I received so many bitter, angry-at-the-industry responses to my screenwriter survey. Their sheer number seems to indicate that there are many writers to whom the immutability of the industry's rules and conventions is not obvious.

Once again, these rules aren't negotiable for these reasons: one, the sheer number of screenplays written versus the number of buyers makes it a buyer's market; two, the entertainment industry isn't a charity or a government agency with responsibilities to you as constituent (other than the Copyright Act prohibition against stealing your work); and three, nobody pleaded with you to write a screenplay.

You do have a bit more leverage with screenwriting contests. Contests see new writers as people to be encouraged as long as you have good manners. They also see you as customers willing to pay the $40 to $60 (or more) feature-script entry fee. So they are happy to accept you as entrants, even if you don't have a chance of winning.

In my survey of screenwriters for this book, one of my questions was:

"If you sent a screenplay with weaknesses to a contest or the industry, did you know any of these weaknesses were there when you sent it out?"

The answers: 21.3 percent "yes," 78.7 percent "no.

That is, nearly 79 percent of those who now acknowledge imperfections in their work did not see those problems when they sent their scripts. They didn't know what the industry expected of them.

As to the other 21.3 percent, who answered "yes" to the question above, here were some of their reasons:

> Because even if I knew there were some weaknesses, it's hard to know exactly where they are, and getting feedback even very critical is part of learning.

> [There was a] contest deadline and [I was] unsure on what needed to be done exactly.

> I didn't have time to rewrite it. I thought any errors might be overlooked because they liked the story and could see it visually.

> I want to get a foot in the door and I hope that the basic good idea comes across and I will meet somebody out there who is able to see that and would be ready to work with me on it.

> I wanted to get it read.

> I was new to the writing genre and subsequently sought professional expertise and was able to correct the mistakes.

> I was so excited that I had finished the script I wanted to know what others instantly thought of it. As it was called a 'rough draft, it was hinted at there were spelling and grammar mistakes. Plus, I am very bad at proofreading which may have been evident in my answers.

> If they were interested in the basic content and concept then rewrites can always occur.

It was the best result I could reach after trying hard for ten years and ending up so poor that I had to turn the page, leave my noisy rathole and get a proper job at least for a while. Also, it's very hard to know when to stop the obsessive rewriting that will lead you nowhere, because nobody cares about your shit anyway...

Lack of time.

No. I paid for several script doctor coverages and incorporated revisions which definitely improved the script.

perpetual problem

This is why I am not submitting to contests.

[I] thought it was solid enough to overlook minor errors.

Time and money. Scripts are always re-written and if a script is in good shape, sometimes you take the risk of sending it in hopes of making a living rather than having it sit in a drawer while you're working a day job in order to keep writing several projects.

To get feedback on direction plot was going.

We could get it working in time before production.

In rewrite I rushed to get it done.

The most common themes I see in the comments above are a deep need or desire for feedback, and a belief that errors and imperfections are not significant and can be dealt with later.

A desire for feedback is an excellent reason to submit a screenplay to a contest, if one is willing to spend the entry fee and settle for very basic feedback.

However, there are better approaches to obtaining feedback. One is to submit to contests which offer more detailed feedback for an additional fee. Another is to retain a script analyst or consultant. Admittedly, either choice involves an expense. The cost of good script analysis averages over $300, which many newbie writers can't afford.

A third is to buy what the industry calls "coverage," which may or may not be sufficient as feedback, but it can be purchased for much less than a full script analysis. Yet another is to pay for what some script scrubbers label as "proofreading," but which often includes notes as well.

It may seem unfair to have to invest in feedback. However, spending money to obtain feedback is a far better approach than sending an unready script to a producer or agent. With rare exceptions, producers and agents don't give feedback. What you will get is a place in their Hall of Shame, a museum where you don't want your art displayed. (More on this in a later chapter.)

5: Crazy, Angry, And Egomaniac Screenwriters

Bad Tempers, Bad Attitudes, Big Egos, Crazy Queries...

...And The Great, Career-Building "Tricks" To Use On Industry People

Just by chance, on the very day that I began to write this chapter, I received this wonderfully illustrative email from a would-be screenwriter (asterisks below are mine):

> Motherfuckers. You creeps stole $20 from me and I want it back. I will do everything in my power to destroy your name and business. Fuck you dirty internet scammers.

Six minutes later, apparently unsure whether his eloquence had sufficiently impressed me, he sent this one:

> Hey thief or thief's accomplice. You're going to rot in hell for scamming all these screenwriters twenty bucks at a time. Maybe it didn't work out for you and now you've got it in for everyone else? You're gonna get what you deserve.

I had no idea what in the world had inspired such classically elegant prose. So I politely asked him to explain the problem.

It turned out that he had paid the extremely low $20 entry fee to a screenplay contest run by a producer friend of mine. He wrote the same nasty email to that producer. He was writing to me because I'd advertised the friend's contest to my email list of screenwriters.

A technical glitch had occurred when he had tried to upload his screenplay.

He had tried to send in his script by email as instructed.

However, this fellow had mis-configured his own personal email server at his personal website (which also wasn't functioning), and so his email server had failed to send an email with the script attached. On that basis, he assumed, as some people habitually do, that everyone in the world but him is a crook, and so the thin layer of mucilage attaching his psyche to society failed of its essential purpose.

That is, he came unglued.

Later, when he came to understand that the entire incident had been due to the mis-configuration of his own email system, he sent emails seeking to apologize. Too late. I had already put his email address into my spam blocker with instructions to bounce and delete, and promptly forgot his name. I can't imagine that any industry person would want to take a second chance with someone who showed such a vicious and stupid side of himself over $20.

In April 2016, another would-be screenwriter wrote to me:

> Thank you for your feedback, I also have feedback for you.
>
> The fact that you so easily and comfortably go into a wildly irrelevant and moronic tirade says several things about you.
>
> 1) You're a coward who hides behind email and would never say those things to anyone's face. Therefore, I propose that we meet so that you can say those things to my face.
>
> 2) You are, an asshole, not only because of your email but also as evidenced by the fact that you've have had numerous jobs (that you can't keep) and also because of how easy it was to find people who will speak off the record about you.
>
> 3) You've been doing this kind of thing for a long time and the fact that you continue to do it shows that you have no conscience about it, this makes

you a depraved asshole.

4) You're a moron, as clearly indicated by the fact that you think "Productions" in a business title automatically means movie or television production.

5) You're an even worse moron (also when it comes to business) as evidenced by the fact that you so easily and stupidly damage yourself by destroying the very relationships upon which your income depends.

6) The fact that you hide behind an anonymous post office box and then throw a childish tantrum when someone does business in that name of a company shows that you're a hypocrite, so basically, ok I'll say it, you're a piece of shit.

* I can't thank you enough for so foolishly showing me these things about you.

*The world is obviously a worse place for you being here, so I have to wonder, what exactly is the justification for your existence?

So what "moronic tirade" on my part caused me to be characterized as a cowardly, depraved moron asshole moron/worse moron hypocrite piece of shit who throws childish tantrums?

I have a screenplay proofreading service. This fellow asked me to proof a single act of a screenplay, a mere $30 job. Then, he twice sent me a non-disclosure agreement he insisted on, without providing any information on who he is. The first time, he provided no identifying information at all. The second time, after I said he needed to identify himself in his own agreement, all he provided was an apparently fictitious* company name.

*Why did I say it was apparently fictitious? The name he gave for his company is not listed as a "DBA" ("doing business as") in his home county. Nor is it a corporation registered to do business in the state. Nor did it have any Internet presence whatsoever. Nor is it listed in IMDB.

Tip to aspiring screenwriters: Producers advise against using phony company names to try to make yourself look impressive. A fake company name will lead producers and agents to conclude that you just got off the long-distance bus from East Bumstead, Iowa with a chicken under one arm and your chicken-poop bingo cage under the other.

In case you're wondering, the identities of both parties go into the first paragraph of contracts; I've signed thousands of business contracts over the years, and this was the first time in my experience that a party to a contract sought to hide his identity.

After these two attempts to get him to add his name in his own agreement (not to mention that we were talking about a mere $30 job), I was out of patience. So I wrote back, "You're beginning to look like an amateur."

Apparently, that statement cracked the thin layer of weak glue attaching this fellow to comity.

I was amused by his attempt to ridicule my work experience ("...numerous jobs that you can't keep."). The fact is that, as of this writing, I haven't had a "job," in the sense of working for anyone, other than being CEO of my own businesses, for 32+ years. Also, the reason I "hide behind an anonymous post office box" is that out in the boondocks where I live, the USPS doesn't deliver mail, so one has to "hide behind" a mailbox, or receive no mail at all. Now, of course, I'm thankful for that buffer, given his "I propose that we meet" comment. I'm sure I don't want to meet him.

Need I mention that no producer would ever want to meet someone who has engaged in such a vile, angry, impliedly threatening rant, either?

So if you wonder why producers worry that the entire lot of aspiring screenwriters, including you, might be dangerously nutty, and why they build firewalls around themselves, the answer is that some of your fellow aspiring screenwriters are creating that impression on your behalf because they are that nutty.

When I started surveying the industry for this book, I honestly thought that my own numerous experiences with behavior as bad as these examples, from clueless and self-destructively rude wannabes, were unusual. Back when I ran a screenwriting magazine, two screenwriting contests, a pitch event, and the world's biggest screenwriting meeting, I assumed that these people felt they could get away with fulminating at my staff and me because they saw us as being on the periphery of the industry, rather than actually in it.

What a surprise when I received the survey results for this book. Producers, agents, contest managers, and others who deal with aspiring screenwriters say that one form of scary behavior or another is directed at them quite often. For example...

> Do not write long query letters with the entire synopsis of your script in one gigantic paragraph that takes up a whole page; that makes you look cray cray. My (standard) response to an unsolicited, and more than slightly crazy, query letter: "Thanks for the query. This one's not for us. Best of luck with it." Writer's reply: "OK. Go fuck yourself, bitch!" – ***Producer, Production Exec/Management***

> After rejecting one screenplay and giving the advice that I was looking for a script that showed The Writer's Voice, the writer was rude, argumentative, and aggressively challenged me on my policy and what my agency should be looking for in writers. His application went no further. As a postscript, the same writer then approached me years later when I was at a different agency, seemingly unaware of our prior contact and the toxic results of rudeness and aggressiveness. – ***Agent; Screenwriting***

Consultant/Script Analyst.

Feedback rebuttal - It's really easy to start arguing with feedback. Never, ever do it ... Don't allow yourself to think "he just doesn't get it" when someone criticizes your work ... I once read a script that I criticized quite harshly. I don't think I was overly mean or said anything that wasn't true, but the feedback was largely negative. The notes I wrote were only a page long. The writer resubmitted a "new draft" (it was barely changed) along with a THREE PAGE document arguing with my one page criticism. Three whole pages of arguments being made about why I was wrong and he was right. Look, if you don't agree with someone's opinion of work, that's fine. You have to know what story you're trying to write. That said, never ever ever do what that writer did. Remember that negative feedback is the best feedback. It's what helps you grow. ... Rule of thumb - if you have to write extra explanation to describe your script to someone, there's a problem with your script. – **Reader for Producer/ Studio/Agent; Screenwriting Consultant/Script Analyst**

Getting defensive about their baby screenplay like it's a personal attack. Don't take advice personally. It isn't your life being discussed and ripped apart but a journey an audience is about to experience. – *Producer, Production Exec/Management; Production manager, sales coordinator for distribution, writer*

Belligerent attitudes toward valid criticism or simply choosing to believe "they don't get it." – *Reader for Producer/Studio/Agent (Former reader for production company)*

1. "I'm a genius, and your industry sucks"
behavior.
2. "No one needs your structure" cliche.
3. Attitude. – ***Producer, Production
Exec/Management; Showrunner***

A half dozen emails with the "updated" script
attached over the course of a few hours is a sign
(clearly) that the writer is not only clueless, but
maybe a little off. When you have to
subsequently say the script wasn't for you and
still needed work and the next email is "What a
gem you turned out to be," you block the email
address and wonder if you should be worried
about being stalked. – ***Producer, Production
Exec/Management***

Once, an aspiring screenwriter in a group got
defensive with my critique, saying I didn't
understand his subtlety or his writing. Other
professionals had made similar comments as
mine, although not as detailed. This writer went
on attack and basically pitched a tantrum. It
wasn't pretty. – ***Screenplay Contest Judge***

Taking criticism of any kind personally and
reacting accordingly. Even the worst comments
by the biggest assholes have a germ of truth
hidden in them and something to offer that will
improve your writing. Be professional. Be
appreciative that someone took the time to read
your piece, no matter how they react to it.
Remember, audiences are as broad as the
population and not everyone is your Mom who
will like everything you do!! – ***Screenplay
Contest Judge, Filmmaker, Writer,
Reader for a Screenplay Competition***

These are far from the only examples. Industry people

cited these behaviors so many times in my survey that I asked aspiring screenwriters in the screenwriter survey to say, in confidence, whether they had ever engaged in that sort of behavior or knew of another screenwriter who had. Here were the questions (screenwriters were asked to check agree or disagree):

Question: "I responded abusively to a contest exec, agent, or industry exec after losing or being rejected."

Answer: Zero (0%) said they had ever done any such thing.

Question: "I took the attitude, 'I'm right/I know it all!' with someone in the industry."

Answer: of the 89 who responded, one (1.1%) admitted he/she had.

However, regarding other screenwriters they knew of…

Question: "He/she responded abusively to a contest exec, agent, or industry exec after losing or being rejected."

Answer: of 91 responses, 11 or 11.1%, knew of someone who had.

Question: "He/she took the attitude, 'I'm right/I know it all!' with someone in the industry."

Answer: of 91 respondents, 21, or 23.1%, knew of another screenwriter having taken that attitude.

One can reasonably draw these assumptions from the above:

1. When a would-be screenwriter goes out of his or her way to be abusive to a producer, agent, or screenplay contest executive (or their readers or contest judges), the event is known only to those directly involved. A producer might mention such an event to another producer, but it's unlikely

that a would-be screenwriter would be dumb enough to tell another screenwriter he had behaved that way. Therefore, the actual percentage who have gone out of their way to be abusive, and the percentage who take the "I'm right/I know it all" attitude, are probably higher than the 11% and 23% whom other writers know about.

2. It's highly likely that some respondents to the survey are being less than frank when they say they have never responded abusively or took the "I know it all/you don't" attitude. If so, that evasion seems reasonable, given the fact that my survey respondents had no way at the time to be sure that their confidentiality would be respected.

Do you wonder why the industry builds walls to keep you out? Look no farther than these sorts of communications from the Stalking Dreadful. People on the inside of the industry have no way of telling who is and who is not infected with this sort of vitriol -- or worse, with the potential for violence.

It Hurts Them, But It Hurts You Much, Much, More

Los Angeles is an impersonal, indifferent, and very large city. It had a population of 10.23 million people by the end of 2016. Like all big cities, it is a place in which bad manners and worse behavior, unless especially egregious, are not unexpected, and are shrugged off as conditions of the urban environment, to be endured, like air pollution.

In L.A., you could insult a stranger in a neighborhood you don't frequent, and the mathematical odds of ever running into that person again are close to nil.

However, the local entertainment industry is not an impersonal, indifferent, very large city. It is a very small town hidden within that big metropolis. It is a town small enough that, while everyone doesn't quite know everyone else, everyone does know (or can quickly find out on IMDB or through connections) about everyone else.

For you, as an aspiring screenwriter, there is no anonymity. There is no hiding. There is no telling off a complete stranger in the industry and never having to worry about having to deal with that person again, or having to deal with someone else who knows how you behaved. When you insult anyone in the industry, you've just lost the parlor game, "Six Degrees of Kevin Bacon."

Hold onto that thought, and consider this one:

A relative of mine, now deceased, founded a private East Coast charity which serves the neediest of the underprivileged. He and others working for him raised nearly $100 million for this charity over the years, offering only one thing in return. That one thing can be summed up in a sentence he spoke to me a number of years ago:

"The world," he said, "runs on thank-yous."

To put it bluntly, all that he offered in return for almost $100 million in private donations to his charity to help the neediest was various and sincere versions and iterations of "Thank you."

The entertainment industry is not a charity, of course. However, it too runs on thank-yous. The movie and TV industry is a small town of people who love to have their work and themselves appreciated. They will remember you for your behavior to nearly the same degree and in nearly the same detail as your neighbors would if you'd spent your entire life in Ten Sleep, Wyoming.

This point seems worth repeating: most of us tend to judge an entire group by that group's worst actors. So when some aspiring screenwriters behave in ways which the industry, or common decency, deems to be unprofessional, many people in the industry will view aspiring screenwriters generally as unprofessional.

The Great "Tricks" To Pull On The Industry Are...

The paragraph above is a fact of life in the relations between screenwriting hopefuls and the industry. It is also a fact of life which you can turn to your favor by employing such clever little "tricks" as these:

● Always show excellent manners to industry people and their staffs. <u>Especially</u> their staffs.

● Always say "thank-you" in person when you have a chance to do so.

● Buy small stationery and envelopes and <u>hand-write</u> thank-you notes to industry people who have given you their time. Even better: order some with your name and contact information at the top.

Given what producers, agents, contests, and their staffs expect from the worst wannabes, your "thank-you" will arrive like sunlight at the end of a hurricane.

6: Are These Demons Yours?
Exorcise Them

More common behavior mistakes of aspiring screenwriters, in the eyes of the industry

Among all the reasons screenwriters fail in the eyes of the industry, this comment from a producer struck a nerve. It felt as if it had been aimed right at a younger me:

> Not experiencing enough life to make a meaningful statement about the human condition.

Why does that comment resonate so deeply with me, and how is it relevant to the present subject?

It made me recall how deeply and how passionately I craved to be a fiction writer in my late teens and through my twenties. The memory remains as vivid as if those days were just last week, not 40 to 51 years ago. I craved to be a "Writer," capital "W," so badly that it hurt. This desire ached in me all the time. I slaved at it. I took all the available college creative writing courses. I paid far less attention to other parts of life – family, college grades, my physical health – than they were due. I even took a low-paid* job as a reporter for a local newspaper because news reporting had been a career path for many real "Writers," capital "W" – that is, people who, as I saw life then, made "meaningful statements about the human condition."

*How low was the pay? I left a night job as a busboy at a diner to take that news reporting job. I had been making 36% more per week as a diner busboy, working fewer hours. That low.

In my twenties, a relative-through-marriage offered to pay to send me to law school. Imagine that: a free law education! As life turned out for me, a law degree might have been a golden ticket to a successful career of another kind. I later spent several years on the staff of the U.S. Senate, advising senators on policy, and now and then, actually writing laws. There were limitations to how high I could rise in that field without a law degree. (National politics was vastly more civilized back then, so a career in the policymaking trade was a lot more respectable than it is now.)

I declined the offer of law school money. No, I wanted to be a Writer, capital "W."

But I didn't. That is, I didn't become a professional fiction writer. I wrote a lot, but got nothing published, other than one story in a college literary magazine. I think I didn't get published mainly because, in the views of editors of literary journals, I had nothing of great importance to say about the human condition.

Twenty years after being first stricken with those first cravings to be a Writer, capital "W," I still had them. I enrolled in film school at the University of Southern California. There, I won three student screenwriting competitions. I believe that I won those prizes in part because, by my 40s, I was closer than younger USC film students to being able to make a "meaningful statement about the human condition."

However, my contest-winning scripts were not quite meaningful enough, or marketable enough, or circulated widely enough, to be sold.

I think that producer's comment explains why many aspiring screenwriters fail. Also, that statement is a more fundamental way of stating many of the other reasons producers give when they say a screenplay is inadequate.

Of course, that phrase isn't the only standard for measuring what constitutes a market-worthy screenplay. Nor is it even necessary to every screenplay. A screenplay which is outrageously funny or extremely scary, or packed with thrills, or which otherwise forms the basis for a very entertaining movie, could be produced without revealing anything of deep meaning. "Ghostbusters," for example. And if its all-female reboot has anything meaningful to say about the human condition, it's not in the content, but in the revelation of the absurd lengths to which hero-worship is taken in the minds of those who were outraged by the idea of a female cast.

However, even if it is not true for all screenplays, that phrase does offers the central clue to why <u>many</u> screenplays fail to interest the industry. Storytelling often fails when one lacks sufficient insight into who we humans are.

For example, in my undergraduate years, I wrote a semi-fictional story about a close friend who died in the Vietnam War. It was based in part on the antiwar letters he wrote to his girlfriend in the three days he was there before he was killed. Despite his antiwar beliefs, he went to Vietnam, and tragically died three days later. My story fudged on the vital, meaningful question of why he went, when his letters revealed that he was so opposed to that war. The story fudged because I didn't know.

I wrote another semi-fictional short story about an incident in my teens. A kid dared me and a friend to bet him $5 that he wouldn't jump off the bridge in the middle of town in Long Valley, N.J. We were sitting on the stone wall of the bridge at the time. From above, the water 15 feet below looked about two feet deep. You could see the trout among the rocks and jagged-edged, rusting junk people had tossed into the river.

The "me" character in the story couldn't figure out why that boy dove off the bridge. Neither could I as the writer. That short story was rejected for publication. The most likely reason was that I didn't understand the question at its core: why he had done it.

I think that sort of insight, or lack of it, is what makes one person a Writer, Capital "W," and another not. The Writer understands why the impoverished rancher Christian Bale takes the job of making sure that dangerous outlaw Russell Crowe gets on the 3:10 train to Yuma, while the "me" watching the kid jump off the bridge into what seemed like two feet of water 15 feet below is merely another gawker, amazed and horrified by the spectacle -- just a reporter writing the events down.

I think a bit about something the TV critic Emily Nussbaum of The New Yorker wrote about the show "Jessica Jones." She made the point that it's not fundamentally about a "superhero," but about a woman who has been deeply wounded by an abusive, manipulative man in a relationship; the "superhero" thing is both metaphor – a shorthand for the depth and incurability of her emotional wounds – and a lure, drawing superhero fans into a story which is emotionally deeper than they probably expected.

If I could squeeze a rule out of the above, it might go like this:

Know why your characters do what they do, on a deeper level than just because the script needs to turn that way. Know why your main character ends up feeling compelled to do the equivalent of jumping off a bridge for $5, or why he puts his life on the line in Vietnam in a war that seems unjust to him, or why one lives a squalid little life like Jessica Jones, battling against crimes done to perfect strangers, or why a farmer chooses to risk his life escorting a dangerous outlaw to the 3:10 to Yuma.

And if you can't, or if you have become too weary to strive toward answers...

Maybe that's why you're not a professional screen Writer, capital "W."

If one accepts the collective views of the industry people who commented for this book, then the creative air from Hollywood to Bollywood is polluted with many mediocre screenplays. You may have the writing skills. You may have learned screenplay structure and the art of visual storytelling. However, if you lack either the insight to say something meaningful about the human condition, or the wit for truly funny comedy, or your horror story doesn't make the reader want to yell to the girl, "Don't open that door! Run!" or if your action-adventure is all explosions and crashes and interchangeable characters...

... Then, like those who can't spell or construct grammatical sentences, maybe you're not yet ready to work at the high professional level the industry demands. Maybe you need more life experience in order to see deeply enough into people and their stories to be a Writer, capital "W." If so, there's nothing wrong with taking a hiatus from writing to gain that experience and insight, or maybe to discover that your real career talents will take you elsewhere.

Maybe, if you have the moviemaking fever but not the screenwriting talent, you should aim to become a producer.

However, let me bookmark this thought for a future chapter: another strong possibility is that your work is fine but your marketing is weak.

Whatever decision you make, you don't serve your own best interests by lashing out at the industry. Be an adult professional, and accept that either your writing to date has not been good enough, or that it is not what the industry wants at the moment, or that your marketing efforts are insufficient, or some combination thereof.

That said, here are some of the other failures of behavior ("failure" as defined by the industry, not by you or me).

"I Know I'm Right And They're Wrong" – The Wannabe's Lament:

In 2013, I surveyed screenwriters for an e-book, <u>The Best Services And Resources For Screenwriters, As Told By Screenwriters</u>. The bulleted comments below, from a respondent to that survey, were among the catalysts for this book:

● He had never taken any screenwriting course of any kind, either from home or in school. In and of itself, that's not so bad–but he seemed genuinely proud of it. He wrote, "I learned by buying the Final Draft software." Did you, now?

● Of a screenplay contest, he wrote: "I even paid about $75.00 for a critique on my screenplay and got a PAS ("pass"?)

.... I know it was a consider or recommend. They never told me what need to do improve action part of the screenplay... dialogue was ok"

● "Did not use a script analyst or consultant's services."

● "I saw part of my screenplay action in the movie called "SUPER 8". The train wreck was my idea..."

● The Nicholl Fellowships competition (according to him) was a fraud. How did he know? "I never got feedback. They never read my screenplay." (FYI, as mentioned in another chapter, the Nicholl Fellowships competition didn't give any feedback until 2015, and still gives feedback only if you pay extra for it. That's not exactly a rational basis for calling the competition a "fraud.")

● "I also wrote another action drama and all I got was that the screenplay to produce would cost about 47 million dollars....I think they only read about 10 to 20 pages and forget the rest of the high action story...My story develops slow and end with lots of action...like a storm settles."

● "I want to see literary agents in person and how they can sign me up. I also have 110 songs to sell to high level singers...most lyrics...Rock and Roll, R&B, Country, Blues, Spanish music, etc."

● "I do not trust Pitch fest. The listener of your pitch steals your idea and create their own based on your idea. The best way is to write your screenplay, get an ET attorney to read it, get a Literary agent and the agent pitches it to the CEO. VIPS of SONY, Dream Works, MGM, Century FOX, etc..."

Well, doggone that Spielberg fellow, stealing your brilliant idea to have a train wreck in a movie. Why, nobody ever thought of that before! So now, you're just going to hire that $600/hour entertainment attorney and pick an agent, who will waltz into the CEOs of major studios on your behalf. And, as he says, the rest is just "etc."

Is it unkind to say that, judging by his complaints and by his language skills, this screenwriter hopeful has made many of the mistakes chronicled in this book? Is it also unkind to say that the worst of these mistakes is the refusal to open one's mind to information which is at odds with one's assumptions and preconceptions?

I'm not trying to say that most aspiring screenwriters are hopelessly mired in self-defeating certitudes and linguistic incompetence, or that most screenwriters try to build careers on the fundament of "I know I'm right, and everyone else is wrong."

Quite the opposite. I think most aspiring writers, like most people seeking to advance in other careers, get most of the rules, terms, and expectations right.

However, some don't. And breaking into screenwriting as a career is so competitive that it's necessary to either do everything right and have a great screenplay, or be extremely lucky and have a great screenplay. And regarding luck, in screenwriting, it's much like luck in scientific research, as Louis Pasteur put it:

Chance favors only the prepared mind.

An Entirely Different "How To Fail" Story...

As mentioned, I was once an aspiring screenwriter. I won the top prizes in three screenwriting competitions at the student level, taking in prize money totaling more than $31,000 in today's dollars. Those were the first three screenplay competitions I entered. Not a bad start. Not a bad haul of cash.

Partly on the basis of those wins, and partly on the basis of having had some interesting life experiences, I landed agents twice by sending out a few query letters. However, neither script sold, and ultimately, I gave up. With the benefit of hindsight, I see three reasons for my failure:

1. I didn't put enough time into it – not enough per week, and not enough years. See Blake Snyder's last blog, in which he comments about Malcolm Gladwell's 10,000-hours rule:

http://www.savethecat.com/todays-blog/best-of-blakes-blogs-blakes-last-blog

2. I isolated myself, even when I did not. In retrospect, this fact seems like an amazing mistake, which I made again and again: While completing my master's in filmmaking at USC and for a few years afterward, I played basketball three times a week at the Hollywood YMCA, where many accomplished Hollywood people played hoops or worked out. Among those on the court with me were a Paramount executive, nearly half the cast of "Full Metal Jacket," a member of the cast of "Platoon," Arsenio Hall, and others. I spoke briefly a couple of times to Jeff Goldblum, who was then a young, rising star, and who exercised there. I nodded at and said hello to Bruce Springsteen in the weight room. A famous actor asked me to go horseback riding with him. I was "one of the guys" among a group of entertainment industry insiders.

However, not once during those years did I so much as ask any of them for career guidance, much less ask any of them to read a screenplay of mine. Not once. One of the producers of a theatrical release, "Miracle Mile," invited me out for a drink. I let that opportunity slip, taking it nowhere.

Why? Lack of confidence in my work? In myself? Thinking that I wasn't ready? All of these. Also, emotionally speaking, I was not the type who asks others to do something for oneself. I blew opportunities because I didn't reach for them.

3. My last screenplay, my best piece of work, was pretty good in its second draft, but it was a strategic disaster. It was based on a true story, a piece of recent American history. It was about race, sex, violence, and the criminal justice system. It had a clear, no-doubt-about-it hero, who took risks and persevered through an escalating series of setbacks to win a significant victory. His victory helped bring about a nationwide change in the criminal justice system – a change arguably far greater than the Miranda decision in the same era. The story would have fit into more than one made-for-TV movie market at the time. Conceivably, it might have even

been a big-screen studio release. The hero of the story and his family were cooperating with me. I had the very last interview with this real-life protagonist before he passed away.

However, In the course of my research, I learned that another participant in the story, one of those charged with the crime, had moved from the East Coast to Los Angeles. So I met with this other man.

I learned in that meeting that he had moved west to tell his own version of the story. His version of events – with himself as the heroic protagonist, naturally – was a sham. He had languished in prison while the man at the core of my screenplay and others saved him. Not only was he in prison, but the triggering event for the entire story was that he'd had sex with an underage girl. He was not exactly hero material. Yet, he was adamant that the story had to be told with him as the protagonist.

With his version of the story floating around, it was unlikely that I could sell a different one; he was, after all, one of the participants, and I was not.

What was my mistake? It was investing so much time and energy, as a brand-new screenwriter, in trying to write a calling-card script about actual events, in which more than one party would want it told his way. In fact, there was another obstacle: the girl, who surely would not have wanted that part of her life dredged up and retold at all. Possibly, if I had first made a reputation in the industry, and become a producer myself, I might have gotten that story made. However, at that time, my standing as an "owner" of the story was slim, and I had no clout in the industry.

Twenty years later, when I was running the <u>Creative Screenwriting</u> enterprise and its contests, one of our contest winners had a similar experience. He wrote a script about a subject which was in the news. Then, shortly after he started to circulate it, a report came out in the trades that another screenwriter had just sold a story about the same real-life events. Those are the risks of a story which is in the public domain. Someone else might be better positioned to write or sell it, or might get there first.

4. Lack of staying power. I probably put in the 10,000 hours which Blake Snyder and the source he was quoting, the brilliant Malcolm Gladwell, in <u>Outliers</u>, talk about. Then, possibly with a breakthrough just around the corner (or just around the next thousand hours – who knows?), I gave up, mentally and emotionally exhausted. My mistake #2 – isolating myself, and having little feedback – was certainly a factor in the sense that I was getting nowhere.

If You Walk, Talk, And Squawk Like A Desperate Loser, You Are One

Another aspiring writer, another incident:

In the 2010 Screenwriting Expo (which I co-owned and executive-produced), a young man pitched a story in our Golden Pitch event. The script was ... Out of kindness, let's call it "underdeveloped." One participating producer at our pitch event suggested that he take it to another company, which was not a participant in our meeting or our pitch event.

This writer then contacted the second company. It offered him a deal which was laughably one-sided. For example, the contract specified that if the company produced the script or sold it to someone else, the writer would then be paid an unstated amount. Meanwhile, this company would own the script, and could oblige him to do free rewrites.

He was furious about the offer. However, rather than just say "No" or attempt to negotiate a more rational deal, he contacted us, raging at the Screenwriting Expo for allowing into the pitch event the company which had, in turning him down, merely suggested that he talk to the other company (which we'd never heard of).

I told him that since he didn't like the deal as offered, he should either walk away from it or try to negotiate better terms. Given how awful his script was, the bad deal he was offered was probably the best he'd ever receive for it without major rewriting.

A few days later, he replied to me that he had signed the one-sided contract without changes. Like the fool who gets murdered in the horror story, all he needed, apparently, was an audience yelling, "Don't open that door!" in order to give himself permission to open the door and plunge though it.

So while I think I made the mistake of keeping myself too cloistered, he made the mistake, in my view, of shamelessly offering bad work to the marketplace without putting in the 10,000 hours, and then the further mistake of seeking people to blame for an offer he didn't like.

Seven years later, he still doesn't have a screenwriting credit.

The Scammer of Contests

Flash back to 2007. As the new owner of the <u>Creative Screenwriting Magazine</u>/ Screenwriting Expo enterprise, I was then in charge of my very first screenplay contest.

A woman entered the contest. She didn't win or even make the quarterfinals.

This made her unhappy. Really unhappy. Cray-cray unhappy.

She first demanded from us that we reveal the names and contact information of the judges who had evaluated her screenplay. When we declined, this woman filed a false complaint with the Better Business Bureau of Southern California, claiming that our screenplay contest was a scam, and that no one had read her screenplay. Her "proof" that we hadn't read it was simply that she didn't win or place high. Her screenplays had placed well in a couple of other contests, and on that basis, she felt entitled to either place well in our contest or publicly smear it as a "scam."

I was astounded. As I was new to the business, I asked the manager of another contest if he'd ever heard of her. Yes, he said. She had done the same thing to his contest. He had gotten her to go away by refunding her entry fee.

I decided not to cave in to this self-anointed victim/bully. I turned the judges' notes over to the BBB, and gave them the judges' names on the condition that the BBB could not reveal them to her. I also did some research on this woman. It turned out that she was the sort of neighbor-from-hell who fought with everybody, and that she had sexually harassed more than one male 30+ years younger than she.

I don't know how many other contests she might have scammed this way, but 10 years later, she has no industry credits, despite apparently having had some talent as a screenwriter.

The industry is a small community. Word gets around.

More mistakes cited by producers, agents, contest managers, readers and judges:

Nagging...

> Sending a draft of the script [to a producer or agent]. Then, the next week, sending another draft. By the third week, they're sending me a new draft telling me to ignore the previous 2 drafts and that this 3rd new draft is the one I should read. *-- A producer*

> Sending email inquiries regarding the status of the read every few days. *– A producer.*

> Persistence that borders on stalking. *-- A producer*

Most producers and agents don't want you to follow up at all. They want you to accept their silence as needing more time and then, at some undefined point, as a "polite pass" – a rejection that is not communicated to the writer.

In my view, the so-called "polite pass" isn't polite at all. It's two things:

First and foremost, it's a defense against the Stalking Dreadful, those crazy would-be screenwriters who think being abusive and scary is a permissible reaction to rejection or honest criticism.

Second, I think it's laziness.

For writers, there is a rational middle ground between stalking a producer with inquires every few days and never following up at all.

That middle ground involves following up. However, some ways of following up are effective. Others are extremely counterproductive. I have more to say on this in a brief marketing chapter below and in a followup book or booklet on marketing.*

* That planned publication started out as a chapter of this book, but when it grew to 50+ pages and still needed more research, I had to turn it into a separate publication or risk never getting this one done.

Cigarettes And Other Vices

> Screenwriters who think they're cool and smoke cigarettes. This is bad for one's lungs. **-- A producer**

> Relying on vice/addictions in order to write**. —** **Another producer**

Do you really think smoking is cool? A 2016 study confirms that people who smoke generally have a harder time finding work – all kinds of work – and are paid significantly less when they do:

http://med.stanford.edu/news/all-news/2016/04/smokers-have-harder-time-getting-jobs-study-finds.html

There are some producers who will not care. However it is unlikely that you'll find any producer who would buy your screenplay or hire you to write <u>because</u> you smoke or vape. So why take a chance that a stinky, disgusting, addicting, extremely unhealthy habit (or its training-wheels apprenticeship, vaping) might cost you a screenwriting gig or a sale, and that you'll never know that it's the reason?

Pants On Fire...

> Willfully lying. – *a Producer calls this the worst*

> Phony resume. – *another Producer*

I would have thought that the above went without saying. However, the fact that two producers brought it up means that there are some would-be writers who lie about their credentials or other relevant information. If you're tempted to do so, consider what will happen when you're caught. Not "if" you're caught. You will be caught.

Another bit of fakery producers don't like, and can easily see through, is that of a screenwriter using a phony company name. It's easy to spot; if a company isn't in the Hollywood Creative Directory and not listed on IMDBpro.com, it's probably a fake. Also, it costs mere minutes (and no fees) for a producer to determine whether you've registered your DBA ("doing business as") or registered as a California corporation.

As I mentioned in the previous chapter, in 2016 a would-be screenwriter went ballistic on me when I wrote that his attempt to get me to sign a non-disclosure agreement with his fictitious company made him look like an amateur. You probably won't be seeing this fellow's work on big screen anytime soon. Faking a company is bad enough; responding with a temper tantrum when one is called out for such fakery is deadly to a screenwriting career.

Is "Show Me The Money" Your Innermost Desire?

> Aspiration to only make money rather than tell a good story. – *a producer lists this as one of his/her "worst"*

Notice the word, "only" in the producer's comment. Of course you should want to make money in the movie business. However, if making money is your only or principal motivation, and it guides your creative decisions, chances are high that your writing will be unworthy of making that money.

About That Catalogue Of Queries You Plan To Send...

> Submitting a 'laundry list' of screenplays, short stories, term papers, etc. – *a producer lists this among the "worst"*

Regarding what and how to query, the advice I read and hear most frequently from people in the industry is to pitch your single best work, and have something quite different (also a polished work) in your back pocket. It may even be a good idea to briefly mention a second, different work down low in the query letter among your credentials (such as, "also the writer of the contest-placing comedy, "My Comedy Name Here") – but don't try to sell that other script in the same query or pitch. Pitch one screenplay per query.

At the same time, you can pitch that second script to other producers and briefly mention the first script down low in that query letter or email.

Is This A Great Idea – "Friend" A Lot Of Producers? Uh, No.

> Soliciting reads and/or production interest via the producer's social media. – *a producer cites this as the third worst mistake he/she has seen*

I ran across a comment at a screenplay marketing website suggesting that you could try to make contact with producers through social media.

That strikes me as a painfully bad idea.

However, there is an exception.

That exception is making <u>proper</u> use of LinkedIn. LinkedIn is not a "social" medium. It is all about business and professional contacts. So if you use a <u>proper</u> approach, it has the potential to be a contact point with a producer. However, the word "proper" is underlined because the right approach is complex and requires a great deal of work.

I did some research on how an aspiring professional in any field of endeavor should use LinkedIn. I will go over this in some detail in my upcoming book/booklet on marketing yourself as a screenwriter. For now, I strongly recommend against trying to use a producer's social media (even LinkedIn, unless you do the research on how to use it without annoying or offending people) to market a screenplay to him or her. The most likely outcome is that you will merely annoy people, and you might get yourself shut out from contact permanently.

Blockbuster-On-The-Brain Disease

> [M]any new screenwriters don't understand the odds their first feature script will be made for over $1 million is next to nil." -- *A producer.*

Some writers of spec screenplays start with the hope, dream, and expectations that their first screenplay will not merely be made with a $1-million-plus budget, but will sell for a million bucks or so.

The reality is that the spec script which sells at all is an exception, and the first script which sells for more than modest money is a rare exception among those which sell. Your psyche is likely to suffer less in both the short and long run if you lower your expectations of selling, lower your expectations regarding the price you'll get, and look at success as the outcome of building a career for the long run.

Are You A Talker Or A Writer?

> Talking about their batshit insane screenplays at cafes while the rest of us work for a living — *A producer.*

Bragging about scripts before they have been written. **-- *Another producer.***

Granted, that first comment is just a wee bit over the top. However, I did develop this "General Rule For Myself About Writers" decades ago, and my contacts with screenwriters over the several years have powerfully reinforced it...

There are two kinds of writers:
One is those who talk about it.
The other kind is actual writers.

In short, the work does its own speaking. The right time to talk about it is when it's finished and you're marketing it.

Marketing "Not Wisely, But Too Well" -- That Is, Like An Amateur

This is a blockbuster that audiences will love! — *A producer, quoting a query letter*

Overselling their work as being 'society-changing' and 'saving the world.' — *A producer/production exec who is also a screenwriter*

In 20+ years of marketing intellectual property, I've learned two vivid and effective sets of advertising and marketing slogans, which are both true and effective:

"Sell the sizzle, not the steak."

and

"Sell benefits."

At first glance, those two sentences might seem to contradict the words of the producers quoted immediately above. Isn't "blockbuster" the sizzle? Isn't "society-changing" a benefit?

No, they're emphatically not.

Yes, you do need to sell the sizzle in your queries and pitches. "This is a blockbuster..." is not the sizzle. Also, it reveals its author to be naive. No one knows at the spec-script stage which movie will be a blockbuster two to four years from now. Also, to the extent that anyone can make that judgment, it is the producer or studio executive, not you, the newbie screenwriter. That sort of comment effectively sells one idea only: that its author is an amateur.

For a producer, the "sizzle" is a unique combination of character and story – a main character who, and a story which, capture the producer's imagination, regardless of whether the movie will save the world or bust blocks.

They're Not Your Mom; Don't Expect To Be Coddled

> ...a needy writer. We are not your mom. We will be respectful but we will not coddle you or breast-feed you while we see what happens to your screenplay. **– A producer/ production executive**

Your relationship with a producer or agent is a business relationship. That is not to say it can't be mutually kind and caring. However, it's not friendship or parenting. It's business.

It is also not an employer-employee relationship. With rare exceptions, you're an independent contractor, and the producer is your customer. That means the producer doesn't withhold taxes for you. You're responsible for paying your own Social Security (and it's twice what is withheld from your paycheck at work); the producer doesn't usually provide you with an office, office equipment or supplies; and you can't charge a producer with discrimination in hiring or promotion or complain to the state employment department about pay or working hours.

Welcome to being an independent business. There are significant offsetting benefits: You set your own working hours and dress code, your morning (or midday or midnight) commute is measured in feet, not stop-and-go miles, you get all manner of tax deductions, and unlike an employee, you own the copyrights to your work until you sign a contract to sell them.

Never Burn Bridges; They're Always Ahead Of You

Again, never send an early or unpolished draft to a producer or agent. Why?

1. You'll Look Like an Amateur Among Professionals. Sending a draft rather than a fully polished, finished work is the first sign that either you're the sort of amateur who doesn't "get" the fact that you're competing with longtime professionals, or that you are unwilling to put in the work. Sending two or three drafts? If I were that producer, I would interpret that as a sign of not only amateurism, but of a scary level of desperation as well.

2. Producers Keep Records On You. The February, 2016 newsletter from Barb Doyon of Extreme Screenwriting revealed this inside secret about the industry:

> "[A] producer may have liked the script, but it wasn't quite right for his company, so he passes on the script, but gives the writer a RECOMMEND," she says. "This opens the door for the writer to resubmit in the future. But the guy who wasted his time with the crappy script gets a PASS for the script and a PASS for the writer. And, <u>most producers like me often write extra notes on our records. I guarantee the producer won't be asking to see another script from this writer, ever!</u>"

That is: by sending out a poorly-written script to a producer or agent, you might be jaundicing that person's view of your next piece of work, and thereby damaging your prospects for a future screenwriting career. Not all producers keep notes on every writer whose work they read, but many do. Don't risk the possibility that not only your script, but you, will be labeled a PASS.

3. They Talk To Each Other. "Being written off by producers in this fashion doesn't seem to bother the wannabe," Doyon adds. "He figures there are thousands of producers and places to market, so what does he care... But anyone who works in this biz knows how small this town is. I can't go anywhere without someone saying they've heard my name! Word gets around...[And] the writer's burning more than producer bridges. There are far fewer reps in town (agents/managers) than producers, and if they run across a producer who tells them you were marketing a PASS screenplay, you're screwed! "

The same also goes for bad behavior, but multiplied. Even if your writing is good enough that your next screenplay might merit a look, bad behavior will put you in that producer's "PASS" list forever, and chances are good that the producer will get word out about you.

But Then, "How Do I Get Feedback?" Answer: Get It Elsewhere

If you need feedback and you feel compelled to send a draft to anyone, then:

- Enter it in contests which offer feedback
- Send it to a good script consultant or analyst
- For a lower-cost version of feedback, buy just coverage or proofreading
- Sign up for a screenwriting class and bring it in for critiques, or
- All four.

You can get basic coverage for as little as $50 if you search the web. Basic script analysis, going beyond coverage, or a proofreader, is available for as little as $150.

However, typically, a good script analyst's work goes for $300 or more (and it can be much more). At those prices, you can expect the analyst to study your screenplay and give you professional, personalized, in-depth feedback.

A further note about screenplay analysts and consulting

services:

The great screenwriter John August, in one of his blogs, dismisses script analysts and consultants. I would not dare to contradict him on most matters involving screenwriting, but on this one, he's dead wrong. I know he's wrong because he was expressing an opinion, while I did the in-depth research he didn't do.

For a book I wrote a few years ago, I surveyed screenwriters, asking about script analysts and consultants. About 85% of the 988 respondents to my survey gave their script analysts a "recommend" or a "strong consider." The survey also asked respondents to grade their script analysts or consultants on a zero to 5 scale. The average score these 988 respondents gave their consultants' or analysts' performance overall was 4.5. Clearly, if nearly a thousand aspiring screenwriters rate their paid script consultants that high, the consultants must be doing something helpful.

Where do you find such a consultant or analyst? You can search the web, and/or download (free of charge) the e-book which came out of that survey:

The Best Script Analysts And Consultants As Rated By Screenwriters

To the best of my knowledge, this is the only reference available on script analysts and consultants. In this book, screenwriters evaluated more than 200 script analysts and consultants. It also lists the specialties (such as particular genres, or TV or features) of most of them.

Caveat: It's a bit out of date. Much of the data comes from a 2010 survey, but some is also from a 2014 update. It is available to you free at:

http://screenwritingcommunity.net/analysts/best.script.analysts.pdf

Feedback Through Classes

Probably the best way to get feedback is to take

screenplay courses in which you can bring in a screenplay and let the instructor and fellow students read it. If you're distant from a college with a good film program, look up and take online courses.

Hal Croasmun at ScreenwritingU.com, and others, conduct such courses online. ScreenwritingU received the highest grades in a survey I did on online courses. However, Hal gets negative feedback, too, which tends to come from new writers who aren't ready for the level of discussion in his courses. So in order to get the feedback at a level you need, choose a course of study that is both within your budgetary reach and within the level at which you need to study.

Vital tip, again:

If your reaction to feedback is that "They just don't get it," then you just don't get it. You'll need either an attitude change or a career change. Accepting feedback is an integral part of the screenwriting life.

7: Copyright Registration? Definitely!

A No-Brainer To Protect Your Screenplay

Afraid To Register From Fear Of Theft?

Caveat and disclaimer: Nothing in this chapter or elsewhere in this book should be construed as legal advice on copyrights or other legal matters. These are the opinions and observations of a writer, not an attorney or copyright expert.

The Writers' Guild of America-West performs a variety of extremely valuable services for its members. It also offers fee-paid ($20) script registration service for non-members at this URL: https://www.wgawregistry.org/ The home page of this service states in part:

> Since 1927, the Writers Guild of America, West Registry <u>has been the industry standard in the creation of legal evidence for the protection of writers and their work</u>. When you register your script prior to submitting it to agents, managers, or producers, you document your authorship on a given date should there be unauthorized usage.

Take a close look at the part of that language which I underlined. Yes, it might well be true that in some quarters, WGA-w registration has been the "industry" standard. However, when it comes to "the creation of legal evidence for the protection of writers and their work," the only truly effective standard is the one the courts and legal system use: the U.S. Copyright Act of 1790 (as amended).

Copyright registration is your best and only complete protection.

Why do I say this? And you might be asking: "What sort of expert are you, Mister Non-Screenwriter Book Author, to be making such a bold statement with such pretensions of authority?"

Let me first answer that second question two ways. First answer: I'm not the only one saying this. See the online articles by entertainment industry attorney Larry Zerner cited at the bottom of this section.

Second, as for how and why I have sufficient experience to comment on this subject, I've been through copyright infringement many times. I've probably won more cash copyright settlements than any Writers Guild screenwriter, current, past, or near future.

Twenty-four times in all, my little two-person writing/publishing company received copyright settlement payments for infringements of our copyrights. The smallest settlement was $300; the biggest was in the range of $300,000 - $400,000. Two other settlements exceeded $100,000. In another case, without benefit of an attorney, I harangued and bullied one of the biggest corporations in the world out of $85,000 for massively infringing our copyrights.

I worked closely with nationally prominent copyright attorneys on the first dozen or so cases, then negotiated 10 of these settlements myself without an attorney. All of our settlements of more than a few hundred dollars were against large corporations.

I discovered and documented the copyright infringements using an Internet software application I created. (It wouldn't work for screenplays; the technical and legal issues were altogether different.)

That is my basis for saying that copyright registration is the only complete protection. It is true that with WGA registration, for $20 you create a secret record of when you completed your screenplay and its content. However, by itself, that record falls short of what you might actually need to protect your intellectual property under the copyright laws.

This is not to say I think you should completely bypass the WGA. To the contrary, spending $20 to register a draft might add a layer of protection, providing proof that you wrote the draft as well as the final version you register with the Copyright Office.

Suppose, for example, that you were to send a draft to someone for comments weeks or months before the script is polished and ready for circulation to the industry, and that person were to turn out to be an unscrupulous thief of copyrights, who then stole it and maybe even had the gall to register it with the Copyright Office. If you deposit that draft with the WGA before sending it to such a person, then your WGA deposit of the draft becomes a record that you wrote it, with a time-stamp before the other party's theft of it. Your subsequent timely registration of the final version with the Copyright Office then gives you all the additional legal protections provided by copyright registration.

Here is are some reasons that federal copyright registration is necessary.

Having filed our copyrights in a timely manner, we were entitled, should there have been a court judgment against the infringer, to two critically important benefits which <u>you will not receive by registering your screenplay with the WGA-w</u>:

1. <u>Statutory damages</u>. If someone steals and produces your work in a major motion picture, then it is likely that actual damages (your lost profits) will be higher than your potential award under the statutory damages provisions of the copyright law. However, if the production resulting from your screenplay isn't a blockbuster, statutory damages (up to $150,000 per infringed work, at a judge's discretion) might be greater.

You need to have the threat of statutory damages on your side. They're a weapon and a negotiating tool for you and your attorney in a copyright case. With this provision of the law, you don't have to prove how much you would have made (which can cost you a lot of money up front for legal discovery and experts). Again: you can't get statutory damages if you don't register the script with the Copyright Office.

For details on statutory damages, see the law on this web

page:

https://www.law.cornell.edu/uscode/text/17/504

2. Legal fees and court costs. The second reason for filing with the Copyright Office, and the most important one in most cases, is that if you do need to go to court, and if you have made a timely copyright filing, you are entitled to court-awarded attorney's fees. If you register with the WGA-w and do not file with the Copyright Office, then, if you win your case, you will not be entitled to reimbursement of attorney's fees. Your legal fees will come out of your settlement. Legal costs could easily consume your entire settlement AND leave you with a legal bill. And that's if you win.

Being entitled to legal fees is huge leverage in a copyright settlement negotiation. An infringing company knows that if it is stubborn, it will end up paying most or all of your legal fees in addition to the damages if you win a lawsuit.

Each of these two provisions of the law provides negotiating leverage; together, they constitute a lot of negotiating leverage if your work as been infringed. They can help you get a settlement without going to court.

The best outcome for a copyright owner is usually to get a decent settlement without going to court. In federal court in California, a copyright case is likely to take three years and cost you a lot of legal fees. (In my biggest case, we sped this waiting period up to a mere six months by filing in what was then known by federal-court lawyers back east as the "rocket docket." However, my little company still spent $46,000 in legal fees.)

All the negotiating leverage is on the other side if you have only registered with the WGA-w and not filed the copyright on time.

To illustrate, here is what typically happens:

Your attorney makes a demand for an end to infringement and for damages. Either you are ignored (a mistake on their part) or, more likely, the alleged infringer's attorneys will look up whether you have a timely copyright filing. If you don't, then that lawyer and client will know that you are in a losing negotiating position because you will have to absorb your own legal costs no matter who wins, and if you win on the merits, you will also have to pay for the complex and costly steps involved in proving what your actual damages are. If you lose ... You don't want to know.

The other side can also figure out fairly easily whether you are wealthy enough to sustain a lawsuit as far as actually getting into court. It's fairly certain that 95% of writers reading this book aren't wealthy enough to take on the legal costs of pursuing a big corporate infringer all the way to winning in court. What the infringing party will not know is whether your attorney has taken the case on contingency (which is unlikely, but sometimes possible).

If you are carrying these twin negotiating burdens – no right to compensation for attorney's fees and no statutory damages – the other side will offer you pennies, or nothing, or drag on the negotiations with your attorney. They'll probably do both in any case, but in the end, you will have virtually no chance of winning a decent negotiated settlement if you have not filed with the Copyright Office.

3. <u>Prima facie evidence.</u> One point Larry Zerner (http://www.zernerlaw.com/) makes is that only registration with the Copyright Office creates prima facie evidence of who owns the screenplay. I asked Mr. Zerner what this means and why it is important. His response:

> ... the copyright act states that registration with the Copyright Office is prima facie evidence of ownership. The Copyright Act does not say that about WGA registration. That's because once you register the work with the copyright office, they have a copy, so people can see what it was that was registered. The WGA does not allow third parties to gain access to what was registered. They only will release the material if they get a subpoena. So, if there was a trial, you could

subpoena the WGA and have them produce the script and prove it's the same. But you don't have to go through that step if you register with the Copyright Office.

4. <u>Why do you want your screenplay to be a secret at all?</u> Mr. Zerner doesn't say this, but his comment points out this vital fact: registering with the Copyright Office makes your screenplay accessible to anyone who wants to buy it (along with, at the same time, giving notice that this screenplay is yours).

You might think, "OMG! But then, anybody could go to the Copyright Office and steal it! OMG twice!"

Pause. Take a deep breath. Now, think that through:

Once you've written a screenplay, you will spend a lot of time circulating it. In doing so, you will have no control whatsoever over where it goes. None. Zero. If you think you're going to control its circulation in the industry, rid yourself of that foolish notion. Your dreams of keeping it secret are defeated the instant you send it to just one industry person or one screenplay contest.

It used to be that if someone wanted to send your script to someone else behind your back, he/she would have to take it to the photocopier, remove the brads, run however many paper copies he/she wanted to share behind your back, collate them, bind them somehow, and then stuff them into envelopes, address the envelopes, take them to the Post Office, and pay to mail them. That labor and cost didn't stop screenplays from being circulated without writers knowing, but they did slow the process down considerably.

Now that your script is digital....Click, click, click, and a hundred people could have it a minute later. Another minute later, they could send it to other people, who could ...You get the picture.

Ever heard of the Blacklist? That group of industry people circulates spec screenplays among its members. Other, less formal, groups do the same. So if your script is good, it gets around, no matter how secret you (foolishly) want to keep it. You should be happy that this is the case. These people who circulate your script are doing your marketing for you. And it's "word-of-mouth" marketing – the best kind there is.

Now, explain to me again why you want to keep your script secret.

Your copyright filing must be timely

What is a "timely" copyright filing? In practice, it should be before you let anyone see the work. Under the law, you have three months to file the copyright after you create the work. However, why would you risk forgetting to take such a vital step on time? File before you circulate it.

Regarding your rights to collect your legal fees and timely filing, see this page:

https://www.law.cornell.edu/uscode/text/17/412

If your copyright has been infringed, hire a copyright-specialist attorney.

Not just any attorney; only a copyright specialist. Do as I say, not as I sometimes did:

I highly and emphatically recommend that if your work has been infringed, do not try to negotiate a copyright settlement yourself. Also, do not retain an attorney who is anything other than a copyright specialist. I hired the wrong kind of attorney just once, in our very first case. He and I were both fools. We settled a potentially very big case (a big corporate perpetrator, nationwide infringement, 25 individual infringements per year for five years, for a total of 125 infringed copyright-registered works) for zero damages. All we got was a company-wide subscription to our newsletter for $3,000 a year.

Thankfully, that same corporate infringer was stupid enough to:

(a) First, go public as a corporation, putting tens of

millions of dollars of public stock purchases in the bank, making it the proverbial deep pocket, and

(b) Then, immediately begin infringing our copyrights digitally on a much wider basis, apparently thinking we wouldn't catch them. They were giving our newsletter digitally 25 times per year to 100+ of their clients. We started losing subscribers, who were receiving our newsletter free, courtesy of copyright infringement.

That was the case we settled for $300,000-plus, using the services of a great copyright attorney. A few years later, another business newsletter publisher, which had a virtually identical case against a big infringing company, won $25 million in a court decision. But that publishing company could afford the legal fees to take the case all the way.

What made me, a layman, enough of an "expert" to pursue ten of my own cases, but not you? Here's what:

1. When I started negotiating settlements myself, I had the benefit of having worked hand-in-hand with attorneys on the first dozen cases. I had all their documents and forms, and I had participated in their procedures. When I needed to send out a demand letter, for example, I knew what to do, and I had a dozen samples in hand.

2. I also had the benefit of years of prior immersion in writing laws as a former policy adviser on the staff of the U.S. Senate. I understood how to look up and read a law. Also, I knew that the legislative history of the creation of the law and the subsequent case law (appellate court and Supreme Court decisions) were vital to understanding how laws work in the real world. I knew how to find these resources and how to read them. Also, understanding and arguing the law are skills I'm pretty good at for a self-trained non-lawyer.

3. I had the time.

4. I had a deeper and more constantly boiling well of fury at the big corporate infringers of our work than you should want to walk around with. I felt violated because they had all signed legal agreements not to redistribute our publication,

and then had gone ahead and done so. They apparently thought that they could get away with stealing from a two-person company which was no bigger than a screenwriting partnership.

5. Catching these corporate thieves was an act of desperation, without which our two-person publishing business would not have survived. We lost 30% of our subscribers to copyright infringement in the first nine months of digital publication, and it was growing worse. I had no choice. You, on the other hand, could take your losses on one screenplay and write the next one. Yes, emotionally, it's hard to swallow that loss. However, we didn't have that option of walking away from these infringements. It kept getting worse.

6. Our cases were factually and legally clear-cut. Corporations with deep pockets signed up for a digital license for one person or a few, and then were distributing entire digital copies to persons and businesses beyond their licenses. The digital tracking system I built caught them red-handed, creating written proof.

Proving that someone took the vital story elements from your screenplay makes for a much more complex case. First, you might have to establish that the infringer saw it, which may not be easy. Second, how much "theft" constitutes actual theft is a complex question with creative works.

So do as I say, not as I did: if your work has been infringed, consult a good copyright attorney -- and preferably an entertainment industry copyright lawyer.

Does It Really Actually Happen? Do Producers Steal Writers' Work?

Not often. However, one of the responses to our producer survey was this painfully personal commentary by a writer-producer:

> Assuming people are always honest, and then having your magnum opus "borrowed" from heavily by a team of publicly respected and well

known filmmakers. (Oh wait, make that a famous producer, writer/director duo, and a mad scientist). Each of whom, at one point or another, proceeded to take credit for the very same script and story concept that went on to become a blockbuster film.

All while the writer watched from the sidelines, knowing full well that only the "unique telling" of a story can be protected. But just because borrowing nearly a dozen very original story elements is not actually illegal does not make it okay. Especially considering that said famous producer held said script under consideration for months before announcing his project. And when questioned by this writer, immediately released the project to another studio ... And the one writer who took him to court and could have won (since he'd actually plagiarized some of her fictitious docudrama material) decided to take hush money and abruptly withdraw her case, and even apologize for her prior accusation.

That's a true war story that nearly destroyed a very decent, honorable person who only wanted to use her gifts to make a real difference in the world. She has managed to move on, and forgive, but how could anyone forget such a thing? Yet, she won't dare speak out, because 1. no one will believe her (in spite of her paper trail) 2. she will be cast as the bitter villain, while the renown ones continue to reap high praise and profit 3. everyone will resent her for speaking out and upsetting the apple cart.

So you do nothing, all while nursing the heartbreak of a mother forced to give up her newborn - to be raised by complete strangers.

I underlined the particular sentences for these reasons:

The phrase, "decided to take hush money" means the real author got paid. If your work has been infringed, getting money should be your main objective. A credit, after a show is released, is usually not a likely outcome. If she didn't hold out for enough, then, yes, I suppose it's "hush money." If it was decent money, then she got paid. If your work is infringed, and you get decent money in a confidential settlement, be happy about that.

Are you feeling a compelling desire for justice? Forget it. Most copyright infringements aren't crimes, so nobody's going to jail. And in exchange for paying you, they get two big benefits: confidentiality and the right to say in the settlement paperwork that they "admit no wrongdoing." When you see "admit no wrongdoing" in the settlement papers, cheer. Combined with a payment, it's corporate-speak for "We're guilty as hell, and you caught us red-handed."

It isn't about being right or getting someone to admit wrongdoing; it's about getting paid and, if possible, getting credit.* It appears from context that the writer being described above didn't get a credit. If a lot was stolen, then a credit might be a benefit worth holding out for (if there is a mechanism to award the credit). If it wasn't a majority of her work, then I'd say take the money and run to your next project.

* I was always outraged when I discovered a corporation stealing our copyrights – I mean, raging around the room, stomping my feet and cursing, daydreaming of violent retribution. That outraged. And I'd stay that way, for months on end. Then, when the settlement was reached, I was suddenly as happy as a clam. All of a sudden, that copyright infringer was my new best friend. When the check arrived, that happy feeling would arise all over again. To me, there is no better revenge in a copyright case than "Show me the money!"

The second underlined section suggests the possibility of either weak legal representation or insufficient courage or endurance on the part of the writer.

I can make that statement about insufficient courage or endurance (and you can't) because I have been exactly in that position many times (and you haven't).

Similarly to producers, the copyright defendants in almost all my cases were holders of copyrights themselves; they were big software companies. My two greatest pieces of negotiating leverage were that they had much more to lose if I went public than I did, and the rage described above.

Based on my experiences, I think the commenter is completely wrong about the dynamics of the publicity. A producer found to have very literally stolen work is at high risk of losing his or her reputation for his/her entire body of work, and is also at risk of other writers' lawyers seeking to pounce. In contrast, if a case goes public, the writer achieves credit through the back door of notoriety. The threat of exposure is a negotiating advantage for the victimized writer. Also, if you ever signal to the other side that you are afraid to go public, you've just lost your negotiating leverage. And probably your settlement.

Yes, it is difficult to be that "little person" going up against a bigger business entity. I did it with legal counsel a dozen times and 10 times without. It is frightening because you could spend money on legal fees and then lose, and if you publicly accuse the infringer of anything beyond the actual fact of the infringement, you could be in a legally liable position yourself.

That is, if the industry's most soulless lowlife dirtbag producer steals your work, you can't call him all those words; you can only accuse him of copyright infringement, and even then, you're only legally safe doing so in a court filing by a competent copyright attorney.

In the case leading to the $85,000 settlement with one of the world's 100 biggest corporations, I was up against an in-house copyright litigator (a staff lawyer who sues others to protect the company's copyrights). I regarded that fact as a small advantage because I figured correctly that she knew the law* and that she had bigger fish to fry, so she didn't want to waste a lot of her time haggling with me. So I made a point of using as much of her time as I could, within the constraints of reasonable behavior.

*If you're right on the merits, the fact that the other side's attorney knows the copyright law is helpful, because she or he will instantly understand the client company's liabilities and vulnerabilities.

My business and I probably would have been in an even more advantageous position if the corporation had hired outside counsel to talk to me. I could have talked and talked and talked and run up the buggers' legal bills to the point at which any settlement would have looked like a bargain.

She offered $25,000. I countered with $125,000. We went back and forth between these two positions for six months. I said I would not take a penny less.

Finally, negotiations stalled. So I said I was going public with my accusations the following week if we didn't get $125,000. I added that she should see the Animal Planet video on the honey badger (this was before Youtube existed). I told her, "I am the honey badger." (If you don't know what a nasty little creature the honey badger is, google a few of the Youtube videos.)

Now, what I actually <u>meant</u> by $125,000 "and not a penny less" was that in my wildest dreams, maybe, hopefully $75,000, and I would have happily settled in an instant for $50,000. Maybe I'd have even settled for $30k --anything more than her offer. When she offered $85,000, I did a silent "Yahoo!" (That's not a hint; the company wasn't Yahoo.)

Fighting an infringer for money takes –

(1) being dead sure that you have the law behind you, which is difficult, to say the least, for a screenwriter without counsel;

(2) courage;

(3) willingness to get angry and stay angry for a long time, then wholly let it go when you win the money; and

(4) the ability to state only facts and threaten nothing but

the public exposure attendant to a lawsuit (which, if you can't even afford an attorney for that part, you can do on your own for about $350 plus fees for motions).

I don't understand why the victimized writer in the situation described above would have had to apologize unless she had publicly said something untrue and defamatory. If you publicly defame someone with false or unprovable accusations, then you're lucky to get away with a mere apology.

Bottom Line:

1. File a timely copyright application with the Copyright Office. Consider also (not instead) registering an earlier draft or the pre-circulation final script with the WGA.

2. If you believe that your work has been infringed, consult an <u>entertainment</u> <u>copyright</u> <u>attorney</u>. Keep in mind that the use of similar or even identical elements might not rise to the level of infringement. It depends.

3. It takes courage, persistence and patience to fight any legal case. I tended to substitute controlled, simmering, self-righteous rage for courage and persistence in our copyright cases, but that works, too – with an emphasis on "controlled."

4. If your work is stolen, it's about the money and, if possible, credit. Not the outrage, not justice, not publicly shaming a producer. Money and credit. Especially money. If you believe otherwise, then I strongly encourage you to adjust your beliefs, or walk away and whine to your friends about your misfortune.

5. Never, ever, ever accuse anyone of stealing your work if the theft doesn't rise to the level of an actual copyright violation. In the case above, both the alleged violator and the alleged victims are anonymous, making this comment very useful for purposes of discussion, but we don't know how much was taken, or whether that actually rises to the level of a legal infringement of copyrights.

For more on why to file with the Copyright Office, see

these online articles by attorney Larry Zerner:

"WGA-w Registration vs. Copyright Registration," by copyright attorney Larry Zerner

https://www.writersstore.com/wgaw-registration-vs-copyright-registration/

"It's Time for the Writer's Guild to Shut down the WGA Registry" (also by Larry Zerner

https://zernerlaw.wordpress.com/2010/12/03/it%E2%80%99s-time-for-the-writer%E2%80%99s-guild-to-shut-down-the-wga-registry/

Caveat and disclaimer: Nothing in the chapter above or elsewhere in this book should be construed as legal advice on copyrights or other legal matters. These are the opinions and observations of a writer, not an attorney or copyright expert.

8: Marketing Yourself And Your Work

A Brief Commentary On Why You Must And How To

These are three virtually immutable laws:

1. As an unproduced, unknown screenwriter, you will spend more time and effort (or the equivalent in money) marketing your work than you will writing it (although see law #3). The screenwriting life will become more predictable if you accept this painful truth now.

2. You can reduce the marketing workload and frustration a bit if you ignore agents until you have a sale pending.

3. There are a few, rare exceptions to the two rules above. Most of these exceptions arise from personal connections, major-contest wins, or the luck of having a screenplay which is perfect for someone at that moment (and in some mysterious manner, such as word-of-mouth marketing behind your back, that someone finds it and is persuaded to read it).

There is an old saying about invention, which applies equally to creative work:

> "Build a better mousetrap, and the world will beat a path to your door." *– mis-attributed to Ralph Waldo Emerson; he wrote something similar, but a lot more verbose.*

Do you believe the screenwriting version of that saying -- that if you write the greatest script ever in a popular genre, the industry will beat a path to your door?

<u>Well, it's wrong</u>. It's not only 100% wrong with regard to inventions generally and screenplays in particular, but it's so wrong that it's a sham, a snare, and a delusion. The world will not divert from its busy path to your door merely because you built the mousetrap or wrote the screenplay.

This is far closer to the truth:

"Build a better mousetrap, <u>and get the word out</u>, and either the world will beat a path to your door, or it will beat a path to the door of the author of a better-advertised knockoff." – **I said that.**

<u>You need to get the word out</u>. If you are an unknown, unproduced screenwriter, it is extremely unlikely that an agent will do that marketing for you, or that a screenplay contest, by itself, will do enough of it for you. (I have more to say on how to use screenplay contest victories in chapter 12 below.)

Here is a success secret which producers didn't mention in the survey and never will tell you:

<u>Create and execute a good marketing plan</u>.

Judging by what I have seen, the single worst and most common failing of screenwriters who (a) have meritorious work and (b) are diplomatic and polite – that is, those who are very deserving of success – is that most are very poor marketers. And in this environment, you need to market yourself or pay someone to do it, or some combination of the two.

"Write script, get agent, make sale"? Pure fantasy, in today's market.

Why Do You Need A Marketing Plan Once You Have A Good Script?

Because you are the suitor, the one doing the pursuing. Because you are one of a hundred thousand vendors trying to sell your product to very few customers. And, as writers say so vividly in Chapter 11 below, your chances of getting an agent to light the way to success and make your noise for you are virtually nil.

Does Commercial Marketability Mean "Selling Out"?

No, marketability is about selling. That's what

professional writers do. It's perfectly possible to be 100% into your story and look to the marketplace as well....[I]f you want to be a pro, then understand what it takes to be one and invest in your writing career strategy.

– Lucy V. Hay, In "5 Wrong Writing Beliefs Holding You Back," http://www.scriptmag.com/features/ask-script-qa/5-wrong- writing-beliefs-will-hold-back-2016#sthash.IfKrvVlg.dpuf

So What Makes A Script "Commercial" or "Marketable"?

I chose Kenya Barris ("**black***ish*") as an example in a chapter above for two reasons. The obvious one was that it took talent, perseverance, and time spent cultivating contacts for him to make it in the first place, and then extraordinary perseverance, on top of talent, to not only make it again, but develop his own network show after his early career had stalled.

The less obvious reason was that he and his work became very marketable in these times.

Who could have known, after what Larry Wilmore called the "ethnic cleansing" – the complete disappearance of African-American shows from TV – that "**black***ish*" would be a hit show, and that several other shows starring African-Americans would suddenly make it onto the TV schedule in the mid-teen aughts?

Well, I could have, at least in general.

Here's why: I'm a publisher (a position similar in many ways to being a producer or very small studio), and therefore, I'm a marketer. I study markets. In the 28 years that I've been a publisher, my marketing staffs and I have managed to sell more than $10 million in intellectual property and information products, such as subscription newsletters, magazines, DVDs, and conferences and seminars to niche audiences.

I have also failed miserably now and then at selling intellectual property when trying to sell to the wrong market, or when the right market was not buying. Just like being told why your script is not good yet, those failures (which cost me a lot of money) were the most painful and best lessons of all.

I couldn't have said exactly <u>when</u> "**black*ish***" might have been a hit, or even which shows would be hits. However, I knew these market facts:

● A higher percentage of African-Americans watch evening TV than any other ethnic group. That is, a captive market was already sitting there at the TV, waiting for someone to put Kenya Barris's work on.

● The lobbying, publicity, activism, and news coverage favoring more minority-based shows had been intense and widespread for several years before his show launched. Eventually, some of the people with production money were going to give in to the pressure -- which, once they did, instantly became publicity in their favor.

● Cable and the Internet have created many more markets for TV shows than ever before.

● Both cable and the Internet have more "budget scalability" than the networks. What this means in terms of new shows (starring minorities or otherwise) is that they can take a low-budget chance on a show, and scale its budget up as audience grows. Or not scale it up. So they do not need to face as much financial risk as network shows. That fact puts pressure on the networks to jump at potential hit shows rather than dither.

Take all those facts into consideration, and I could see that it was inevitable that one outlet or another would produce a show or two or three or more about modern African-American families, and/or an African-American-dominated drama, and that something would be a hit.

This is not rocket science. It is true, as William Goldman has famously said, that nobody knows anything for <u>certain</u> when it comes to predicting winning shows. However it's possible, listening in on the society around you, the world, and their news, to spot and write for social trends as they emerge.

For example, in my screenplay proofreading business, I read a TV pilot which focused on campus rape. In my view, this pilot had all the story elements which should be there, given the way that this issue has been thrust into the public consciousness and conscience. The writer sees it as a potential network show.

However, you might be asking, "Isn't campus rape a subject too narrow to sustain a dramatic TV series?"

Well, yes, in my opinion, it is. However, while the pilot episode is about rape, the series is about the full social life of a college campus. The writer wisely introduced other current university-campus issues and built the story around a character who works at the university rather than around only students, who (one would hope, anyway) move on to the next phases of their lives.

In other words, the writer combined that which is vividly in the news and public discourse with a solid cast of characters, especially the lead. She also briefly introduced other college-campus themes and issues. In addition, the writer chose a fairly obvious target market, and the writing avoided such network no-nos as overt sex or bad language. If written for, say, Netflix or HBO, it could have been a bit more raw.

In my view, this is a writer who is writing both to be "real" -- that is, to say something meaningful about the human condition -- and to sell.

Many writers who care deeply about the content of their work seem to be emotionally unable to transform themselves into the roles of sideshow barker, used-car salesperson, or multi-level-marketing huckster.

And that would be a good thing if it weren't getting in your way.

However, judging by the comments from the industry,

thousands of others scribble shallow and meaningless trash, then jump right into marketing, bringing to mind a comment from writer/producer Barb Doyon in a prior chapter:

> ... the guy who wasted [the producer's] time with the crappy script gets a PASS for the script and a PASS for the writer. And, most producers like me often write extra notes on our records. I guarantee the producer won't be asking to see another script from this writer, ever! ... Being written off by producers in this fashion doesn't seem to bother the wannabe.

This chapter, and my next book or booklet on marketing, are intended for those of you who take the time and make the effort to write screenplays which are both worthy in content and polished in grammar, formatting, and structure.

It is often repeated that:

"I can't get a sale without an agent,
and I can't get an agent without a sale."

The good news is that this widely-repeated, defeatist view is not really true. You can get an offer from a producer without an agent. And then, you stand a better chance of landing an agent to help negotiate that deal. Alternatively, you could retain an entertainment industry attorney to negotiate or at least review the deal.

Yes, You Can Market Yourself – And It Works

With all the resources available today, you should be able to do a better job of marketing yourself and your work than any agent you'd be likely to land if you are a new, unproduced screenwriter.

The "how-to" of all that is far too much to cover here, so I'll say this:

You can take charge of your marketing (and many screenwriters do), either by paying for some of the existing marketing resources, or doing the marketing work yourself, or best, some combination of the two.

Good marketing is a source of great power. If you market effectively (and, of course, if the work is worth buying, both on merit and commercial viability), you can generate more than one offer for a feature screenplay or pilot. By doing both your market research and your marketing well, you will have a far better sense of what your options and opportunities are.

Then, if offered a deal you don't like, you will have the confidence to decide whether to give in and sign it or keep marketing. If you do sign it, you will do so knowing either that it's the best available offer, or that you are taking that deal because you don't want to put any more effort into marketing that particular screenplay. Then, you can move on to the next screenplay, knowing you got the best deal at the time for that one.

Easy for me to say, right, having never sold a screenplay?

Yes, it is. I've researched just about all of the marketing approaches and methods available to you as a screenwriter. In the course of that research, I noticed that they are not significantly different from the marketing methods I've used for many years. The tools of marketing are basically the same everywhere. And if done well for a worthy and properly targeted product or service, they work.

If you don't want to wait for my upcoming booklet, be encouraged to do some research yourself on ways to market yourself and your work. For example, a proofreading client of mine sold a screenplay very quickly on Inktip.com.

Several screenwriters have found paths to sales through schools and classes, such as the online and phone classes given by Hal Croasmun at ScreenwritingU.com; you can read more at the website.

Some writers obtain referrals to producers by having industry-connected script consultants and analysts read their work. I know and deal with a number of those consultants and analysts. They have legitimate contacts in the industry.

Screenwriter friends and other screenwriters I know personally have gotten sales or work by winning or placing in contests, then marketing themselves.

The Writers Store publishes a helpful book on producers and agents to contact.

The Done Deal Pro forum at http://messageboard.donedealpro.com/boards/ offers both suggestions and critiques on various ways to market your screenplays and yourself, and comments from people on their successes and failures with various approaches.

There are many other approaches.

The one marketing approach I don't have any faith in is "Get an agent." It could take years to land one, if you do at all. Then, the chances are fairly high than any agent you do land as an unproduced screenwriter will do a weak, insufficient job of marketing on your behalf. I had agents twice in the 1980s, before I founded a publishing business and had to quickly teach myself the basics of marketing. What I could see in hindsight, after learning how to advertise and market my work, was this:

The two agents I had in the 1980s did mediocre jobs of marketing me and my work. Most likely, the reason was that these agents thought my scripts weren't really good enough, or their subjects "hot" enough, to merit greater effort. But possibly, they were both just lousy marketers.

A Fact Marketers Know, Which You Probably Don't:

What do screenwriters do to self-market (not counting paid services)?

Typically, they write a query letter or email. That is, <u>one</u> query letter or email.

Then, they sit and wait, quivering with anticipation. Then, when winter sets in, they sit quivering because they're freezing and can't afford the heating bill because they haven't sold anything.

What does a marketer do that is different?

Every good marketer knows that it takes several successive ads, often with different core appeals and approaches, to sell anything. That is, you don't write and send "a" query letter. You write and send a series of them.

Take time to notice, for example, the marketing war between Geico and Progressive to win you as an insurance client. It is virtually impossible to watch TV for hours and not see commercials from both. If you go to the movies (at least at my local theater), you'll also see Geico commercials before the movie starts. Repetition (if and only if done well) sells.

A word of warning, however: A bad multiple-contact approach, and a multiple-contact approach for a bad script, are two of the surest ways to get yourself blackballed in the industry. You do not want your brand identity to be "Not HIM again!"

The Last Word In This Chapter:

Get the word out, or sell nothing. The only marketer you can count on, day in and day out, is yourself.

9: Writers' Complaints About the Industry

The Writer Survey Questions

As previously mentioned, after reading the views of the industry about screenwriters, I sought screenwriters' views on the way the industry treats you. I wanted to see both sides of the dialogue more clearly. That survey was titled:

"The Movie-TV Industry: What Is Going Badly For Screenwriters? How Could It Be Better?"

The Survey Questions:

Respondents were promised confidentiality, and were asked these questions:

1. ABOUT PRODUCERS: What's wrong with the way production companies, or a particular producer or production company, treat aspiring screenwriters, or have treated you, and what could and should they do differently?

2. ABOUT AGENTS: What's wrong with the way agents and agencies, or a particular agent or agency, treat aspiring screenwriters, or have treated you, and what could and should they do differently?

3.ABOUT SCREENPLAY CONTESTS: What's wrong with the way a particular screenplay contest, or contests generally, treat aspiring screenwriters, or have treated you, and what could and should they do differently?

4. Any other industry person or type you want to complain about?

The survey was closed after receiving 129 responses. I don't regard that number as a statistically valid sample. However, it seems valid enough for illustrative purposes, and with four questions multiplied by 129 responses, it's a big batch of anecdotal data. The survey results are offered and discussed in these chapters:

● Chapter 10 is about how producers treat aspiring

writers.

● Chapter 11 is about how agents treat aspiring screenwriters.

● Chapter 12 covers aspiring screenwriters' views of contests.

To the extent that my views in the following chapters seem jaundiced or harsh, I apologize in advance for any offense given. However, my comments to writers in these chapters are an attempt to state, as clearly as possible, the realities of the marketplace for screenplays as defined by the people who have the power to recommend and make the buying decisions.

10: Aspiring Writers' Complaints About Producers

And Why The Most Frequent Complaints Are Dead Wrong

This chapter recites and discusses the complaints of respondents to the screenwriter survey about producers and production companies.

The question was:

> "ABOUT PRODUCERS: What's wrong with the way production companies, or a particular producer or production company, treat aspiring screenwriters, or have treated you, and what could and should they do differently?"

The responses – Complaints About Producers ...

Complaints #1:
"They Only Make Franchises, Remakes, Comic Books, Star Vehicles..."

> Production companies seem to be too keen to buy something which is immediately sellable. They are obsessed with "IP's", sellable property, which they can buy. They should instead be more focused on talent and the development of ideas and/or people.

> They are looking for fluffy things.

> Investors read screenplays and judge quality with no understanding of the craft, arc of the character, etc.

> Production companies are afraid to take a chance on anything new, so they just keep recycling the

same old stories that have been done numerous time. Not all classics should be remade.

Only dealing in/see franchises and do not consider original ideas.

Some of them pretend they're "indie-friendly" and willing to read unsolicited material, but they just want to look cool and will never actually spend time on anything coming from a complete unknown. If we could make a list of them, it would save us a lot of pointless efforts.

Lean too much toward formulaic plots, focus too much on producing films based on established properties like TV shows, comic strips, toys, cartoons.

Too commercial, only interest in money.

There is a great deal of re-hashed garbage out there.

They will consider and/or produce sheer garbage if they think it will make money.

The sincerity of these comments is vivid and quite touching. One can see that, to a degree at least, they arise from a desire to write meaningful scripts and see them produced. The frustration, the umbrage, and even bitter despair running through them are obvious, and, I'm sure, heartfelt. However, I see two problems:

1. They're demoralizing to anyone who buys into them.

2. <u>Very little in these statements is true</u>. Yet these beliefs are stated, widely and often, and are just as widely nodded at, as if they were lumpy little pearls of woebegone wisdom.

Some of them are true to one degree or another, but in large measure, they're not true. Here is what is true:

1. In a typical year, 700 to 900 movies and TV pilots are produced in English.

2. It is impossible to draw any one set of aesthetic conclusions which accurately describe the content of this entire body of work, much less the conclusion that most are fluffy, garbage, franchises, star vehicles, "IPs," or made only for the money.

3. The biggest audiences at movie theaters are children, teens, and very young adults. Why is that? Because –

4. Young people want to go out and tend to go out, and it is these young people who are the biggest audience at the multiplexes where most tickets are sold. Older people tend to stay home and consume their entertainment on TV. This is relevant to this discussion because –

5. Items #3 and #4 explain why a high proportion of the movies which make their way to the mall multiplexes are indeed fluffy or "garbage" (in the eyes of those who presume to be artistically or intellectually superior), franchises, star vehicles, IPs, and made principally for the money. Those are the movies this biggest audience segment buys.

Also, that which may be "fluff" to you is bright and new to tweens, teens, and young adults. Life is new to them, and every generation absorbs the same lessons about love and life anew. This particular generation happens to absorb many of those lessons through graphic novels.

Complaining about which movies make it to the malls is a bit like complaining that your local supermarket sells red meat and the auto dealership sells gas-guzzling SUVs. Maybe everyone should be a vegetarian and drive a pint-sized hybrid, but in a free society, people get to make their choices.

When screenwriters make comments like those above, the subtext I read is:

> "I want my screenplay up there on the big screen
> at 3,500 theaters nationwide, and I don't care to
> have my dreams disturbed by the fact that the

biggest audience won't buy enough tickets to make it worthwhile financially for those who have to put up the money."

It is not dictation from the studios which determines what plays in your local theater. It is the ticket-buying preferences of the predominant theater-going audience.

I communicate with my local three-screen theater owner all the time about what he plans to show. For example, he chose to exhibit "Hillary's America: The Secret History of the Democratic Party." Why did he screen that piece (which I view as mental sewage)? Because local people of conservative views engaged in a write-in campaign asking him to. That is the democracy of the marketplace in action.

He didn't screen "Dope" or "The Birth of a Nation." Why? Because those films are principally attractive to two audiences – African-Americans and liberal-leaning, highly educated, NPR-listening, Huffington-Post-reading whites – and there are few residents of either description up here in the mountains where I live.

"The Birth of a Nation" received the most buzz at Sundance in 2016; it is hardly what one could call "fluff." But did it screen at your suburban mall multiplex or small-town three-screen theater? If your town is mostly blue-collar white people like mine, then, almost certainly, it did not. And I had to drive 40 miles down a mountain road to see "Dope."

Again, is that because some invisible hand of the studios prevents these movies from being shown at my local three-plex? No, of course not. It's because the local audience wouldn't buy enough tickets to financially justify exhibiting them here.

Compared to the number of movies made, the volume of what you might be inclined to label as studio "fluff" or studio "garbage," et cetera, is relatively modest. This is easy to demonstrate by looking at the statistics on what is produced. Below are some sources which show the true picture of what is being made. These facts, and even more, the lists of productions they represent, show just how wrong you can be about what is produced (and about what kinds of screenplays are sought) if you're looking only at the top of the box-office charts.

Admittedly, the biggest paychecks do go to the writers of the scripts the biggest audiences attend. We all want the big bucks. What the authors of those comments would need in order to make their big-bucks dreams come true is a different paying audience. The theatrical audience would have to be people with more sophisticated or mature tastes, or at least tastes friendly to the sorts of screenplays they write.

"But," you may feel compelled to argue, "if they only made movies for a more sophisticated audience, then the audiences at the malls would change."

Yes, they would. They would be a lot smaller.

It is the customer, not the maker of the product, who does the choosing and sorting-out of where movies play. In business, as a publisher, I have learned similar lessons about publications the hard way, more than once.

Numbers And Kinds of Movies Being Made:

Independent (That Is, Not Studio Releases):

The website thefilmcatalogue.com allows the visitor to search for independent films by many criteria (by year, by genre, by status, by language, et cetera). When I first wrote this paragraph in early 2017, it listed:

176 films in pre-production
204 in production
179 in post-production
199 completed (that is, completed in 2017 alone).
Of these, about 84% are in English.

This catalogue is not all-inclusive. It includes the sorts of films which are brought to the annual American Film Market, the biggest exchange in the U.S. where independent producers try to find distributors for films not released by major studios. You can use this catalogue at no cost to see what is made. You'll see a great variety of stories.

There are other film markets similar to the American Film Market. The biggest annual marketplace for movies and TV shows in Europe these days is Marché du Film, the commercial complement to the Cannes Film Festival, where about 3,200 producers from around the world try to sell their films to 2,300 distributors. In 2016, there were 1,450 screenings of films at Marché du Film. The Toronto, Sundance, Austin, and other film festivals around the world are also marketplaces, at which award-winning movies are often picked up for distribution. Very likely, few to none of those would be fairly labeled as "fluff."

Releases: A Partial Look

All of the films and TV shows in the stats above had scriptwriters. However, not all had the good fortune to have found distributors which will exhibit them in major-chain movie theaters. Here are two sources of statistics on films released:

Theatrical Releases By Major Distributors:

A partial list of films released for theatrical distribution in 2016 can be found at the URL below. The total number released into theaters in this list is about 274, down from 320 the year before:

https://en.wikipedia.org/wiki/2016_in_film#2016_films

https://en.wikipedia.org/wiki/2015_in_film#2015_films

Home Video Releases

You can find a partial list of films and TV shows released onto home video in 2015 and 2016 at the URLs below. Among the movies, there is some overlap with the list above of theatrical releases, but many were not released theatrically. I didn't count, but between movies and TV shows, these partial lists are several hundred per year:

https://en.wikipedia.org/wiki/2016_in_home_video

https://en.wikipedia.org/wiki/2015_in_home_video

Film Festivals: A Way To See The Real Movie Business In Person

"Just beyond the glare of Hollywood's blockbuster-movie spotlights is one of the world's highest concentrations of film festivals," wrote Dan Allen in the September, 2016 issue of Westways, the magazine for Southern California AAA members. His article listed 50 film festivals in Southern California alone. Among them, they screen hundreds of independently-produced movies each year.

There are hundreds of other film festivals in the U.S. and around the world. They're easy to find at the websites filmfreeway.com, withoutabox.com, and filmfestivals.com. If you still think the bitter comments made by writers above paint an accurate picture of the movie and TV entertainment industry, your eyes will be opened by attending a few film festivals. Again, if you live in Southern California, that Westways article lists 50 within driving distance.

Film festivals can also be a way to market yourself and your work. (But not by simply showing up with a script and/or a stack of marketing literature. It's more complex than that. I'll have something on using festivals for marketing in my upcoming marketing book/booklet.)

Film Freeway and Withoutabox, in case you didn't know, are also two of the best ways to search for screenplay contests; both accept entries for hundreds of contests. An even better way to search for contests, in my view, is this Moviebytes.com page, because it shows scores and rankings from prior contestants:

www.moviebytes.com/contests.cfm?category=Upcoming

Bottom Line: Hundreds of Independent, Non-

Blockbuster Movies Per Year

So...

● hundreds of films in English in thefilmcatalogue.com;

● 3,200 producers courting 2,300 distributors at the annual Marché du Film;

● the November, 2016 American Film market had about 700 screenings of 400 new films which were seeking distributors;

● several hundred movies and TV shows released onto home video per year (some are old shows, but most are new work); and

● hundreds of festivals per year screening independent films.

Yes, some of these movies and TV shows are the sort of "fluff" or "trash" these survey respondents complained about. However, if that is what you believe, you're disparaging the paying customer, not the producer.

If It's Not True, Then Why Is "Everyone" Saying It?

In a comment cited elsewhere in this book, a screenwriter said studios "groom" audiences to accept these box-office-leading movies. Others said basically the same thing. Movie critics, especially (whose collective knowledge of film markets is about as vast as their knowledge of Cuneiform) tend to spout on this theme.

Again, this is factually upside-down. The real "grooming" that takes place is the young audience telling the studios what to make for the big screen. There's a great article on this very subject, "The Mogul In the Middle," by Tad Friend, in the January 11, 2016 issue of The New Yorker. It tells you exactly what a studio chief (in this case, the chief exec at a new studio, STX, which is trying to inhabit a place in the market between the sequelitis/franchise studios and small independents) does to justify making $10 million a year. His most important job as chief executive is to figure out what multiplex audiences are going to want to see two years from now.

The 2016 Labor Day weekend box office take offered a vivid illustration: "The Light Between Oceans," a serious love story for adults, was heavily advertised, but did a weak $4.9 million at 1,500 screens in its opening weekend, while "Don't Breathe," yet another iteration of the scary-guy-in-the-dark-house horror sub-genre, did $19.6 million on 3,000 screens in its second weekend, earning $55 million in just 10 days.

In other words, the studios did their best to persuade customers to buy tickets to "The Light Between Oceans." The result: "No, thank you."

So if these views on "grooming" audiences are not true, then why do some aspiring writers subscribe to them? Here's a reasonable theory:

The authors of these comments haven't sold anything. They're unhappy. They regard their own work as more in-depth and more "serious" than that which they see on the screens of the multiplexes, where a fair percentage of movies fit their negative descriptions. (Don't we all take our own work seriously, and feel just a pinch of jealousy when someone else's work, whose faults we can see more easily than our own, corners the big bucks? Of course we do; that's human nature.)

They may feel a deep emotional need for some external excuse for working so hard at screenwriting without success. And there is no price to pay for espousing such views anonymously in a survey. So they don't bother doing two minutes of research on what is actually being made, either because it didn't occur to them, or because that research would refute the comforting "blame the producers/studios" explanation for one's own lack of career progress to date.

Is Blaming The Studios Or Producers Working For You?

Do you think the studios groom audiences to accept fluff? If your answer is "yes," is that working for you?

Probably not. In fact, it could be exactly what is holding you back. In order to succeed, you need to see the business as it is: many productions, many more outlets (between big and small screens) for productions than ever before, many genres and sub-genres, many more scripts sold as pilots or to independent feature producers than ever before, many miniseries made, and only a few big-budget blockbusters made.

Then, you need to figure out where you fit in. That is, you need to figure out where the sort of work you write is exhibited and who produces your kind of work. This is fundamental marketing research.

If there was ever a golden age for screenwriters, it's now. There are far more buyers of movie and TV screenplays than ever before, and that number has been growing in the past few years.

If your screenwriting career isn't working, give a good deal of thought to whether your marketing outreach is both sufficient and appropriately targeted. Objectively consider the quality of your work. Also, consider whether your work is of a genre and format which smaller producers are buying. Consider whether you have adopted a defeatist attitude or you're fatigued from the effort made so far, or afraid of rejection, any or all of which might be holding you back. Consider whether you're suffering from a combination of these factors. To succeed, let others be the pessimists.

Take heart from the fact that the total number of productions per year is a thousand or more (and the number of scripts purchased or optioned is more than that). Take heart from the fact that the creative variety and vitality of all these productions in any year defies simple description, especially the description, "commercial," when it is used in a disparaging way.

"Commercial" is a good thing for your script to be. I've never heard of a producer who gathered millions of dollars together to make a movie with the intention of losing it all.

116

"Only" Interested In Money? Then Why Are They In This Biz?

Certainly, producers and the rest of the industry are more that just "interested" in money. They crave it and they thrive on receiving a lot of it. They have to be: Making movies and TV shows is expensive and risky. A producer has to spend $250,000 (microbudget) to more than $100 million (major budget) of someone else's money turning a screenplay into a production. No producer (or screenwriter, for that matter) stays in the business long with a money-losing track record. However, most producers are in this business mainly because their passion is making movies and/or TV – for the art, the fame, the public adulation, the respect of their peers, or whatever combination of motives – just like you. Not solely for the money.

So what is the rationale for spending that sort of money if the industry sees the story as a losing bet? There is none. To write for the entertainment industry, one must write something which is polished and brilliant, and which also has a chance of fitting into one commercial niche or another. Writers with talent, soul, and passion, and who also come to terms with these realities, are the ones who endure.

Complaint #2: The So-Called "Polite Pass"

"I feel that the "no answer" is a bit disappointing. Instead of just saying "this script is not for us" or "we don't have time to read it", they just never say anything, which is a bit disheartening. Perhaps some website where they could filter through all the requests they get would be helpful :-)"

"Several times there is no response and you are expected to consider it a "pass." More contact via email would be beneficial."

"Never hearing back - even if they have invited you to submit."

Yes, that hurts! However, that silent, so-called "polite pass" is the way it works much of the time. I don't like it, and I don't see any reason you should like it. In my view, a producer who agrees to read your script (again, he/she didn't ask for it; he/she agreed to your request to read it) does take on the responsibility to show you the courtesy of a response. That means communicating "No, thank you," when the answer is "No, thank you."

However, neither your wish nor mine is going to change the way it is. One reason for many producers' use of the "polite pass" is that some would-be screenwriters respond badly to rejections. Producers and their staffs are people with feelings, too. They don't want to suffer the harangues, the curses, and the argument that "you just didn't get it." Choosing not to respond is the simplest way to avoid confrontation.

Also, they didn't ask you to write your screenplay. Therefore, from their perspective, they are doing you a favor by reading it. So rather than fight it, take the so-called "polite pass" as the ill-mannered norm. However, one thoughtful producer made this helpful suggestion in a survey response:

> A recommendation. Follow up with a company you've submitted to once. Then calendar it for every three months, with a letter or an email. I personally prefer letters because I get more emails and they sit on my computer screen annoying me until I can get to them. If you feel you have to call, make the phone call, but don't give attitude to the receptionist if we haven't called you back in the time frame you've set. She just answers the phones, it's not her fault I'm busy.

This producer is unusual in one regard: he or she does let writers know if their scripts are rejected by his/her company:

> If I don't call you back, it doesn't mean I've lost interest in your work. As soon as that happens, you'll know immediately because I will let you know immediately. If I do decline you, it's not a good idea to

tell me off and let me know how sorry I'll be. You may want to submit to me again, and there's a good chance you'll submit to someone I know in the industry and they may just ask if I've heard of you.

Complaint #3:
"They Should Reach Out to My Age Group, My Ethnic Group, My Gender..."

> More companies should make opportunities readily available for young writers, female writers and writers who are of different nationalities.
>
> And forget about making anything with more than 3 people of color in it. The industry only is looking for the white male/female 18-25. The US, the world is made up of all kinds of people.
>
> As a ethnic minority, African American, I would like to see greater outreach to potential minority scriptwriters.

I, too, would like to see more diverse, more believable stories. Reaching for that better, more diverse content would necessarily involve seeking a more diverse array of writers, including female writers and African Americans (and older writers, a group most of you younger advocates dismiss as if we did not exist).

There is good news on this front for women and minorities. To a degree, that which you pray for is trending, at least at the moment:

> Over the past year, shows like **black**ish, Empire and How to Get Away With Murder helped usher in a new level of entertainment-industry interest and confidence in shows featuring more diverse actors in key roles. Some people even expressed concern that the industry might overcompensate for years (decades) of lack of diversity with too

much of it in the next TV-pilot season. Gasp! (Is too much diversity even a thing?):
– Akilah Green, in a Sept. 15, 2015 article on 15 new TV shows with African-American leads. **See the article at:**
http://www.theroot.com/articles/culture/2015/ 09/black_stars_shine_in_15_new_tv_shows_w orth_watching_this_fall.html

Writers of color aren't the only people with valid reason to complain, and who are seeing at least some degree of change. Several female comedy writers and comedians have been getting shows recently. Their work is vividly real and their subject matter is trending. Amy Schumer, for example. Chelsea Handler. Samantha Bee's weekly comedy show, recently profiled in <u>The New Yorker</u>. Sharon Horgan ("Catastrophe" and "Divorce" on HBO with Sarah Jessica Parker in the lead) is also a rising star who was recently profiled in <u>The New Yorker</u>.

Complaint #3a:
Aspiring Older Writers Feel Left Out, Too...

> Possible age discrimination. If you're an older screenwriter and not established, once your age is apparent to the producers they may think of you as not connecting to a youthful demographic.

> I have found many producers and industry workers to be age prejudice. Some of us might be old, but that should not be held against us.... Life experience can only be gained from living. If the story is good but our language is dated, <u>hire an editor to fix it</u>. Don't just scrap it because we're old.

Being "Medicare-eligible" myself as I write this, I'm quite sympathetic to the argument for giving a fair shake to older writers. I suspect that I'll even turn "old," whatever age that is, before too many more decades pass. Based on my own experience (I founded and grew a successful publishing company and then raised the money and acquired and ran another, in part because no one would hire me), I believe there is a great deal of truth to the accusation that older writers tend to be dismissed without a second thought.

That said, however, do I smell the whiff of an excuse in the phrase above, "...but our language is dated..."? I'm not sure what is meant by dated language. I still write in basically the same language as when I started writing for money five-plus decades ago. Could it be that the commenting writer's language is either grammatically incorrect or weak at description and dialogue rather than "dated"?

And writer, if your language really is dated, then: Dog, are you saying you're too old to learn new tricks?

If your script isn't right in some way, you need to make it right before you send it out again. The industry doesn't owe you, individually, any special consideration solely because you're in or approaching my age group or, for that matter, because you're pleading for special treatment on the basis of being in any other audience group whose grievances deserve redress. Other people in your group, whatever it is, have the skills and are putting in the 10,000 hours.

As mentioned above, Kenya Barris wrote 19 pilots seeking to have a show of his own – <u>after</u> he had once made it and had then left a show. Just as discrimination against you is wrong, so is discrimination in your personal favor ahead of the talented minority or female or older or whatever-your-group writer who has the storytelling and language skills and puts in the effort.

I underlined "hire an editor to fix it" in the older writer's comments above to reiterate a point made in an earlier chapter, that you (or a professional screenplay editor/proofreader you hire) are that editor. Correcting your work is your responsibility; the industry didn't ask you to write screenplays, and doesn't owe you an editor.

At the same time, there is hope for the older writer. Hal Croasmun of ScreenwritingU regularly offers a free phone-in class, "Screenwriting Over 50," dealing with the hurdles older writers face. For details, see: http://screenwritingu.com

Complaint #4:
Producers With Narrow Ideas And Tiny Budgets

Some of the requests/want ads from producers for scripts you get through marketing organizations are so specific and narrow-minded they are ridiculous, like: looking for scripts to be shot in the North Pole about ninja turtles. Some of these so called producers have such tiny budgets, you need a magnifying glass to see them, i.e. looking for a sci-fi in the vein of Aliens or Starship Enterprise but under 5k. Really? So that means you are paying $50 for the feature film.

The fictitious example is certainly ridiculous, to be sure. If you feel so negative toward those requests, then do bypass them. No one is forcing you to send your screenplay to an aspiring producer with a narrow idea of subject matter or a very small budget.

On the other hand, if a producer specifies a lot of detail in the sort of script she or he is seeking, then it seems highly likely that she/he has the money or sees a path to the money to make and distribute that story. If you don't like the story, fine; however, those specifics might well mean there is a path to a production credit for the writer who can write that story.

On another other hand, everybody starts somewhere. John Sayles wrote a cheesy little horror film called "Piranha" when he was getting started. A then-unknown director, Joe Dante, made a name for himself directing it. Ben Affleck directed "I Killed My Lesbian Wife, Hung Her on a Meathook & Now I Have a Three-Picture Deal with Disney" in 1993. Francis Ford Coppola directed movies of the "nudie cutie" genre. In fact, his "Peepers" was in some vital and obvious

122

ways a precursor of what was to come with his brilliant "The Conversation." See:

http://flavorwire.com/372522/the-embarrassing-early-films-of-oscar-winning-directors

I'm not saying that cheesy work is "the" path into the industry. But it is one path.

Complaint #5:
"They Decline To Read the Work of Unproduced Writers"

...without an agent or rep, having one's screenplay read by anyone with production resources is extremely unlikely. This is true of both TV and the film industry.

They generally don't consider the work of writers who are not known to them. Also, if you are the wrong age or sex or have the wrong zip code-- forget it!

There are very few film producers in my area. I would like to be able to find some in my area to network with.

Do not accept unsolicited material. They should at least look at a PITCH page before rejecting an idea.

Some will refuse to read the script if it is not from an A list screenwriter. There are also some subjects they will not take a chance on at this time.

Companies need to be able to be more flexible and also very clear on what they want.

Producers in general are of the opinion that they

are doing you a favor by even looking at your work. This same behavior (haughty and egotistical) even occurs if your work is either optioned or bought, they are doing you a favor, so you should be honored for the exposure (and don't talk to us about financial recompense). A person needs to be connected in some way if you want to get noticed.

Many production companies seemed closed to new works or writers. Many have their own writers on their payroll and will only use those individuals.

They tend not to want to read anything except by established talent.

If you are signing a release form, more producers should be willing to read your work. The readers should be willing to provide some feedback to you, as well. If you've taken a year or so to write a script, they can at least make some suggestions or referrals, then they would create more partnerships in the industry. Some people may have great ideas, but their writing level may not be quite as polished yet, but if the producers could still work with you and negotiate something, then it creates a win-win situation. In the end, I think they would get an increase of better, and more creative projects.

I would hope that production companies can look into projects from aspiring writers as samples to judge their writing and how well a writer can formulate and construct ideas. Or even a writer may forward a slate of ideas to judge that part. I also hope that production companies can look to grow aspiring writers who haven't gone to Film School etc, to work up their productions from low-budgets to blockbusters. Whether in-house or having the position to refer a writer to other companies or producers. I know it may be difficult but on the long run, I think it will increase productivity and the quality of films we'll see.

Yes, it is true that most production companies and virtually all agents say they don't consider queries from, or read screenplays submitted by, unproduced writers who are unknown to them and lack representation.

So what's the lesson here for the aspiring screenwriter who wants to succeed, given the barriers the industry puts in your way? Give up? Or are there creative and clever ways for the determined screenwriter to get around the Great Wall of "No"?

First, it pains me to say this, but to the writer who complained, "They should at least look at a PITCH page before rejecting an idea" and others who feel that way:

Again, the harsh reality is that the entertainment industry has no obligation to read your work, your pitch, your query letter, your anything. I know that angers and frustrates you. When I wrote to the office of the legendary Swifty Lazar back in the mid-1980s, my envelope was returned unopened inside a bigger envelope. Wow, was I insulted and furious! How dare they not even open the query letter I had taken the trouble to write?

Well, not only did they dare, but they had a perfect right not to read my query or screenplay. And somehow, Swifty Lazar managed to have a legendary career as an agent without ever reading a word of my work (which seemed impossible to me back then; I, too, had a bloated and fragile screenwriter's ego).

Nowadays, the memory of my belief back then that Swifty had a responsibility to read my work (because how could he possibly get along without it?) seems pretty amusing. That is, in moments when it doesn't feel downright embarrassing.

Neither you now, nor I back then, have or had any entitlement to claim the time of producers, especially those who specifically say they don't want to see your screenplays. <u>Having said that, however</u>...

There is plenty of reason for hope

First, those who make clear and firm rules also make quiet little exceptions. If you have the right stuff,* you have nothing to lose by sending your script to producers who produce that genre and format of your story, but who say they won't read material from unrepresented writers. With that right stuff*, some closed doors do open just a crack.

*What's the right stuff? This entire book is about what that phrase means. However, to put it into a few words: your work is of a genre, theme, trend, and format which that producer seeks; your grammar and formatting are excellent-to-perfect; your work is vetted; it is mature, strengthened by the sort of rewrites you can do only after receiving good professional feedback; you and your work have credentials (such as significant contest wins, or it's based on your piece of fiction published by a major publisher, or it has "recommends," or you lived the experience, et cetera); you are always assiduously polite, diplomatic, and thankful; and finally, your marketing materials are polished and your marketing efforts are sufficiently extensive, patient, and diligent.

As for being unknown: You can change that. You can become "known about" by winning contests, by pitching, by optioning or selling scripts, by building a track record of credits, however small, by getting yourself listed at IMDB.com, and through effective marketing of well-written, highly original screenplays ...and by showing great manners.

More on Your Manners

I cannot over-emphasize the value of showing exceptionally good manners to the entertainment industry. Most screenwriters do not write "thank-yous" or exhibit any exceptional, memorably positive manners to producers when rejected. They just take their rejections quietly and go away. Some act like self-important jerks, and a few are outright vicious. Unfortunately, it is these jerks and nasty people who set the level of expectations the industry has of aspiring screenwriters.

However, that expectation creates an opportunity as well. Showing exceptionally good manners sets you apart. You will be remembered individually as neither part of that silent, possibly grumpy majority of the rejected, and absolutely not one of the jerks.

Finding Producers Who Will Consider Your Query

Some producers and agents do seek screenplays from unproduced, unrepresented writers. There are multiple ways to find and contact them. The Hollywood Screenwriting Directory, published by the Writers Store (writersstore.com), lists many producers and other industry people who will consider the work of unrepresented, unsold, unknown screenwriters. They are a minority, but a large minority. There are also many fee-paid services and venues which help screenwriters contact producers, agents, and managers who are otherwise out of reach.

As for being from the wrong location: In what industry is this any different? If your passion is to design BMWs, you move to Munich, Germany. If you want to brew Coors, you go to Golden, Colorado. Design the next iPhone? Plan on moving to Cupertino.

It is not impossible to get a first sale in the movie and TV business from a distance, especially if that distance is Toronto, New York, or the neighborhood around a good film school outside of that amorphous geography known as "Hollywood."

However, if you want a screenwriting career, you probably will have to spend some years where the business is. Generally speaking, only screenwriters with a track record of success can move beyond "Let's do lunch/Take a meeting" distance and live wherever they want. With very few exceptions, the successful screenwriters whose addresses I know live in the Los Angeles area.

> ... subjects they will not take
> a chance on at this time...

Yes, that is true. When was it ever not true? Is it necessary to state the obvious, that a movie producer has to make money or his or her business will close, and its employees will be out on the street? Making a movie or TV series is expensive and risky, and every competent producer has a far better idea than you do of what he or she can obtain financing for. They are not going to buy your argument that they should take greater risks with their and their investors' money based on your judgment rather than their own.

I know that this is difficult medicine to swallow, and I do feel for you. However, your work has to be something which a producer sees as a money-maker.

Regarding this comment from above:

> [Producers act as if] you should be honored for
> the exposure (and don't talk to us about financial
> recompense)

My thoughts: I don't know the particular details the screenwriter is complaining about, but generally speaking, if you don't like the deal, negotiate. If the producer won't budge, decide whether to take the deal or politely decline and seek a better deal.

I do realize that many writers are afraid to decline a weak offer and move on because they fear that there no other offer will be forthcoming. If you can't generate a better offer, then one or both of these possibilities is true:

● No one else sees the screenplay as being commercially viable at this time.

● You haven't marketed it widely enough, long enough, or effectively enough.

As for the comments:

> Some people may have great ideas, but their
> writing level may not be quite as polished yet...

and

> ...if the producers could still work with you [and]
> ...grow aspiring screenwriters...

There are several programs, some run by studios, which do work with emerging writers. A screenplay proofreading client of mine applied for entry into one of two emerging writers' programs at NBC/Universal. Others submit to Amazon Studios; their work goes through a critiquing and suggestion process from other writers. The Sundance Institute has a fellowship program for screenwriters. Disney/ABC has had a fellowship program. So do CBS, Fox, Nickelodeon, the Cinestory Foundation, New York Women in Film and Television (see http://www.nywift.org/article.aspx) and others. There's a list of diversity writing programs at this Writers Guild of America west web page: http://www.wga.org/the-guild/advocacy/diversity/writing-programs-conferences-festivals

Also, the Nicholl Fellowships is a screenplay contest leading to paid fellowships for the winners.

However, entry into all of these programs, and others, is competitive.

Did you find yourself agreeing with these two italicized comments above? If so, was that because you did not know that such programs exist? Or do you believe that some unpolished writers (perhaps yourself in particular?) should be entitled to a spot in one of these or other writing programs, or even a writing position with a producer, without having to compete with the hundred thousand or so other aspiring screenwriters?

If your answer is the latter, then on what basis do you

make such an argument, other than a sense of entitlement?

It would be great if there were more such programs. I'm all for it. However, five or ten or twenty more training or fellowship or writing internship programs would mean that only five to maybe 100 more writers, out of 100,000 or so, would find places. The situation would look no different to those of you who don't find these programs and apply.

I think that it is fair and just that generally, those who are less capable should not be chosen over the more capable. The existence of programs for minorities and female screenwriters is not at all inconsistent with this view. These programs seek to overcome the real and perceived biases in the predominantly white male producing and studio exec ranks. However, entry into any of them is highly competitive and rightly so.

So if you believe you could thrive under a mentor, apply.

From the perspective of the industry, relying on talent and developed skills, as opposed to choosing a screenwriter who is less capable or unproven, is also the practical and financially safer course. Once again, entertainment is a business, not a social services agency or government program. Entertainment companies must make profits to stay in business.

In addition, helping you and other aspiring writers to take ideas and turn them into polished screenplays is exactly why there are film and TV screenwriting programs at colleges, online screenwriting courses, screenwriting seminars, evening screenwriting classes, other educational programs, screenplay consultants, dozens of "how-to" screenwriting books, and videos, and hundreds of online "how-to" articles.

Given all the programs available to help you develop your skills, and the fact that thousands of other writers invest the time and money to learn, it seem a bit unrealistic and selfish to expect that the industry should make a special accommodation for you personally.

"A slate of ideas..."

> Or even a writer may forward a slate of ideas to
> judge that part. I also hope that production
> companies can look to grow aspiring writers who
> haven't gone to Film School etc.

A slate of ideas, rather than writing the screenplay? After
reading that Kenya Barris wrote nineteen pilots (after he'd
already worked on TV shows and was then out of work, and
that he was raising a family with a wife in medical school at the
time), that statement drew this reaction from me:

Either it arises from unawareness of just how hard others
work at it, or it's just lazy.

Also, as a practical matter, a slate of ideas tells the
producer very little of what he or she really needs in order to
evaluate a screenplay.

Moreover, suppose you do submit an idea which a
producer likes. Given that you have not written the screenplay,
the producer will most likely react, "Wow! Great idea! I'm
going to pay (fill in name of that producer's favorite available
professional) to write it!" You'd be out of luck. Bare story ideas
cannot be copyrighted, only a particular expression thereof. If
you think an idea of yours is worthy of a screenplay, write the
screenplay. You're competing against a hundred thousand or
so people who are taking the trouble to write their screenplays.

Regarding the second part, wishing that production
companies could "grow aspiring writers who haven't gone to
Film School etc.," the commenter seems to be making the
argument that someone who hasn't made any of those efforts
to learn should be selected by a producer ahead of those who
do. Few people in the industry, if any, will accept that
argument, and I see no reason they should.

Complaint #6:
"Readers For Producers Don't Know Good Scripts"

> Not many producers get to see scripts. It seems
> that is for assistants and sub assistants to

address if they see fit.

The main issue is the process of getting the material into a producer's hand. Unless you know the producer, the script invariably is gatekeepered through a lowly, overworked and abused Reader (who frequently, but not always, has little knowledge of story and character development). However, given the number of aspiring screenwriters (good and bad, but a tremendous amount of bad) pounding on producers' doors, I see little alternative.

The maze of the studio/corporation based entertainment industry seems to be constructed to give people jobs whose job is to just say no. The people with the least experience about scriptwriting are the ones who read the scripts and they are too afraid to recommend things because if their boss doesn't like it, it bodes poorly for them.

They hire incompetent readers. Example I put ONE camera direction in a script because I thought it was important to the character, and was severely marked down by one reader but not the other. Result was the company passed on the script.

Yes, many production companies hire readers to review scripts before they're passed up to a producer. That is a fact of the screenwriting life, and it's not going to change. Moreover, I have never seen any basis for believing that a script which a reader rejects would receive more favorable treatment from the reader's boss.

Calling script readers "lowly" and saying that a reader "has little knowledge of story and character development" are disparaging remarks. No doubt, they arise out of the frustrations of being a screenwriter. Yes, your frustrations are genuine. However, blaming screenplay readers is pointless. Indeed, if you believe that a producer has hired an incompetent reader, aren't you saying that the producer, too, is incompetent because he or she, who uses the services of this supposedly incompetent reader on a regular basis, can't tell that?

Typically, script readers are formally trained in script reading. Also, they are trained by their employers to watch for that which the employer is seeking. One comment above claims that readers are "afraid" to pass scripts up the chain of command. If I worked as a reader (which is similar to working as a screenplay contest judge, which I have done), I would be "afraid" to recommend the sorts of scripts the boss has said he or she doesn't want to see. It's not being "afraid." It's having the sense to heed what the boss wants. In what line of work is this not the way it is?

How To Game This System And Win

The "how to succeed" lesson in this instance is that you are not going to change the way the system is structured. So, rather than complain about it, your task is to charm the reader with a great logline, a great pitch, and especially a great script – and to expect, and deal diplomatically with, rejections.

Also, as I mentioned in the chapter on copyrights, very good screenplays which don't fit at one company are often circulated to others. That is how the extremely "inside" and influential Blacklist (https://blcklst.com/) began, with readers and producers circulating to each other the screenplays they liked but their companies weren't going to produce. The founder, Franklin Leonard, turned that informal process among insiders into a formal organization, which will now let you list your screenplay for a fee. From the Blacklist website:

Non-Guild members must host at least one screenplay or pilot ($25/ script/ month) in order for their membership to be active. We also encourage, but do not require, the purchase of at least one paid read from our readers ($75/read for screenplays and pilots >= 60 min, $50 for pilots <= 30 min).

There are other, less formal pathways than the Blacklist by which great screenplays circulate around the industry. That process is very much alive.

So if you have a great script, have courage. Get it out to producers who are interested in that kind of work. Some readers or producers might show it to their friends at other production companies or agencies.

My thoughts for the *"ONE camera direction"* commenter:

Yes, it does seem harsh and extreme, if indeed your screenplay was rejected because it had but one camera direction. However, it is more likely that your script was rejected for other reasons. If that camera direction was cited as a reason, then most likely, their real reasons were more difficult to put into words, or they were more harshly critical of your work, and you were being spared those harsh words.

Complaint(s) # 7:
Demands For Free Rewrites; No Pay Or Deferred Pay

> I'm tired of people trying to get something for free from me. That goes pretty much across the board.

> Since I am between agents, it is difficult for me to get access to people who actually have money to pay me to write. Some people expect screenwriters to work for free or on a deferred basis. I make my living from my writing (fiction, screenwriting, and even technical writing). In no other industry would anyone expect someone to perform a service without payment or deferred payment (if the project sells). Although it sound as though I'm only in it for the money, I am not. It is a matter of respecting someone enough to compensate them for their services.

> Most producers seem to think that writers

should work for free, including multiple rewrites, until and unless the project is produced.

Screenwriters should also be paid for what they do and not be ripped off.

When producers ask for free work, in my case the completion of four episodic scripts, with no game plan or even flat rate, it's incredibly vexing. They also expected scripts to be written with no series bible, no official showrunner or polished pilot. This situation arose from an independent film production company with clearly zero television development experience.

I can only partially agree with these views. In some industries, such as the tech industry, ground-floor participants in startups often work for future compensation and stock, which can make them either millionaires or broke and cranky later. Poets and emerging short story fiction writers often work for nothing but publication. Writers of nonfiction and fiction books rewrite and rewrite and rewrite and rewrite (etc.) between rejections without pay.

How does the tech industry compare to the entertainment industry? In this way: Every new movie or TV show is a new startup business. If it's financed by a Writers Guild signatory company or even a big non-signatory company, then the production company already has the money in place. Such people shouldn't be asking you to bear any of the risk or burden; they should buy your script.

However, smaller, independent producers are not usually so fortunate as to have production money in place when they see a script they like. Until there are investors, the producer is probably working for free, living on his or her past income from another project.

At that pre-funding stage, the writer and the producer are two independent businesses. You're dealing with a partner-to-partner or contractor-to-subcontractor relationship. In some cases, an independent producer can afford to buy and pay for the script outright. In others, the producer pays for an option and then tries to package the deal with lead actors and a director to obtain financing. However, at some other times, the producer asks the writer to share the risk that the project will succeed or fail by asking for free rewrites, seeking a free option, or offering deferred pay.

It is difficult for many people who get paid regularly in their day jobs, and who think like employees, to deal with and accept this status of independent, risk-sharing business partner. It is not difficult for me to understand this point of view. This book is a venture, and I haven't had a job as someone else's employee since 1984.

For productions which are not made under the agreements of the Writers Guild, some degree of risk-sharing is common, legal, and an acceptable business practice.

This is not to say you have to like such deals. You do have choices. You can accept a deal of that sort, or you can walk away and seek a better deal elsewhere, or you can try to negotiate for more money later if and when the project is financed, and maybe also another paycheck or points if and when it is produced or distributed.

When a writer complains about being asked to share the risk, it usually implies that the weak offer is the only offer he or she has received. This, in turn, implies that either the screenplay is not seen by others as commercially worthy at this time, and/or that the screenwriter hasn't marketed it well enough to receive better offers.

Judging from my years of interactions with screenwriters, insufficient marketing is typical. Marketing oneself and one's screenplays is foreign to most aspiring screenwriters. Most of you seem never to have imagined before you started writing that marketing was more than an afterthought to the writing. Marketing is often the more strenuous part, and often takes more hours and more months of the aspiring screenwriter's time than writing the script does.

Regarding the situation described above in which a writer was asked to complete four episodes, I probably would have either said "No, thank you" to that request, or counter-offered a different deal.

My reasoning is that writing four episodes on spec seems like an excessive expenditure of time, especially when writing them for a producer with no track record in TV. However, rather than say "No" outright, I might have made a counter-offer something like this: Make me one of the executive producers, with a big cut of the producers' pay if the show sells, and I'll write four episodes. Or: I'll write one pilot episode and a brief series bible.

If the basic idea were my own (the author of the comment doesn't say whose it is), and if the producers were to say "No" to making me a partner, I'd move on and market it elsewhere. If the story were theirs, I'd say a polite "No, thank you" to doing all that writing, other than asking to be made a producer or under this possible exception:

I might work for deferred pay, or for a credit only, if I were a newcomer with no decent credited work yet. In such a situation, I'd also look at these two vital questions:

1. Do the would-be producers seem to be very good at what they do?

2. If it's my script and if I don't take this deal, am I going to make the effort to fully market it?

The element that most aspiring writers don't consider in such a situation is that marketing oneself requires developing some expertise and then doing a lot of work, over a period of time. So is it better to accept a mediocre offer now, or counter-offer while continuing to shop the script around? That's up to you.

Complaint #8:
"Mr. So-Called Producer"...

Anyone can call themselves a producer, but few

know what a good script truly is.

To be a screenwriter, you have to have a script. To be a producer, you have only to want to be a producer. Thus, they can hunt down scripts anywhere, including places like InkTip, with no money, no contacts, no real plan, and waste hours, days and months of a screenwriter's time with zip to show for it. Too many wannabe's who don't know what's required to actually make a film. Wishes are not anything tangible. I have a script. What do you have, Mr. So-called Producer?

Certainly, a screenwriter should be cautious and do all due diligence before accepting an offer or a proposal to work together from someone with no credits or industry history.

However, in order to succeed, you might want to stow away the attitude displayed in the comment above, listen to that "Mr. So-Called Producer's" sales pitch, and show that person perfect manners. Then, decide later, after giving it some thought and obtaining advice, whether to take the deal. Never burn a bridge, because in this business, all burned bridges lie ahead of you, not behind you.

For example: suppose the person with no credits or industry experience has just graduated from a program like the Peter Stark Producing Program at USC. When I was at USC getting my master's in filmmaking in the 1980s, this program was both the best of its kind in the country, and also the one most connected to the domestic industry. It might still be; I don't know. And suppose this no-credits producer is gung-ho and has a deep craving to produce a movie or TV show, and is excited about your script. In the situation I've described, are you, as one of 100,000 screenwriting wannabes, really in a position to take an attitude like that of the italicized comments above, and dismiss this person out of hand?

I think not. That "Mr. So-called Producer" is in pretty much the same position as the unproduced screenwriter.

Having one of 100,000 or so scripts on the market does not automatically make you better than he is. Getting a better offer is what puts you in a higher position in the industry.

To put all this into a paragraph: To succeed, drop the attitude. Consider all offers. Take the best one which offers you a simple way out in case it doesn't work, or turn down that offer and continue marketing. Go into any meeting with an open but wary mind. Yes, you might well be taken advantage of. It is also possible that meeting "Mr. So-called Producer" could be the break of your life, the start of your great screenwriting career.

In any case, do thank "Mr. So-Called Producer" for his time and any notes he might give you.

Also, regarding people listed as producers on Inktip.com per se: Inktip has a qualification process for being listed as a producer. Credits are required. The comment above is inaccurate with regard to Inktip.

Complaint #9:
"Writers Are Treated As If We Were A Dime A Dozen"

> In my experience, producers believe screenwriters are a "dime a dozen" and don't need to be treated with respect.

No additional details were provided.

It is no surprise that unproduced, unknown, unrepresented screenwriters can feel as if the industry sees you as being worth a dime a dozen. I think it would be more accurate to say that until you have proven yourself to the industry, you are one of many hungry outsiders looking in, and people in the industry have full schedules and mouths of their own to feed. It's a long, hard road to being valued by the entertainment industry, and most aspiring screenwriters never make it there. I'm sorry to have to point that out. Even so, a producer should show good manners, just as you should, and if he thinks you're a dime a dozen, he should keep that attitude to himself.

Complaint #10:
"Why Isn't There A Free Online Database Or Pitching Service?"

I have found that it is quite hard as a new writer that I don't really have a track record so it has been a struggle to be able to find the right Industry person/company. I think what troubles me the most is that there are so many of us out there that though we may have fabulous work, we just don't have "Industry" access, and therefore, finding an agent is utterly impossible as a new writer. Therefore, I am very thankful for online companies such as INKTIP and VIRTUAL PITCHFEST. Though, the reality is that we as new writers, and unknowns have to "PAY TO PLAY" but at least this allows writers such as me to get in the game for a price, and have a chance of a little bit of access to the INDUSTRY. PAY TO PLAY at least gives us a window to get our work somewhere, even if it is an Indie company with a small budget or an up and coming agent, producer or manager -most likely at entry level in whatever company that they are working for. The internet has enabled unknown screenwriters to have a few choices to get their work out there, and I think that this is the wave of the future in how we get our work picked up, the only downfall /negative is that if you are a screenwriter without the funding to buy pitches, or buy listings, you are at a disadvantage. Therefore Online pitching/listing/query services are wonderful, but at the writer's expense. It would be wonderful if there was a site much the same as FACEBOOK, where it didn't cost anything to list- that you sign up with a free account, though I don't know how that would work, but it would be ideal.

Also if production companies would have an online platform for spec scripts to be submitted such as Amazon Studios.

The author of this comment acknowledges the value of marketing outlets like Inktip.com and Virtual Pitch Event, and thankfully, in my view, does not express a sense of entitlement to a free script listing service, saying only that it would be ideal for screenwriters. However, I've run into other wannabes who do feel that they should have access to a free pitching site.

Yes, such a site, like all free stuff, would be ideal if it worked. However, questions come to my mind. The most obvious is who, other than screenwriters, would be motivated to pay for it? With such an oversupply of screenplays and screenwriters clamoring for attention, certainly the industry has no incentive to pay for such a database. In fact, Inktip partially addresses this question in its FAQs:

> Not charging industry pros for this service works to the advantage of writers, by helping writers to sell more through greater exposure. Charging industry pros would result in drastically fewer of them visiting the site to even look for any scripts. (For example, a car dealer who charged customers just to come look inside his showroom wouldn't make many sales, would he?)

Complaint #11:
"They Hype The Dream To Screenwriters"

When I went to a screenwriting convention I saw too many people trying to sell the dream of screenwriting to novice writers.

Yes, it happens. A lot.

When I ran the Screenwriting Expo, the biggest annual screenwriting meeting in the world at the time, some speakers use their sessions to hype their services. Selling paid services to screenwriters does indeed involve hyping the dream of screenwriting to novice screenwriters.

However, is it not also true, from the very fact of your attendance, that you already had sold the dream of screenwriting to yourself before you showed up at that convention? If not, why did you go? So are that speaker and that meeting really overselling the dream, or are they merely preaching to you, the choir?

The latter is more true, I think. Let me add this:

You face great challenges. Therefore, in order to succeed, you need to cling to a statistically unrealistic level of hope. You need to dream ridiculous, impossible dreams. You need to continue to try when your fingers and mind are too weary, no matter how hopeless ...

That is an absolute necessity in order to succeed as a screenwriter.

Yes, a bit of that sentence is blatantly borrowed from "The Impossible Dream" from "the Man of La Mancha," but it's true. The odds against you are virtually hopeless. But if your work is good and your heart is kind (and you're not an incessant whiner), ignore the odds. Keep writing. Keep hyping the dream to yourself.

Or quit for now. Live your life. And then, maybe come back to the dream later.

Complaint # 12:
"The Screenplay Is As Important As The Stars"

> I think an area where producer falls flat is seeing a script as a blue print and not as a work of art itself. Seeing the screenwriter as lower than the movie stars. A great script is just as important to a movie as a big star. You may not market the script to the public but I think a great script will make more money than a bad one. Sure, some

awful movies are made that succeed at the box
office but I still think that if you have a great
script it has a better chance of success.

I wouldn't try to argue that a great script is NOT a work
of art. However, I wonder whether the author of this comment
perhaps overestimates the value of the screenplay in relation
to the collective value of all the other artists whose work goes
into a movie: the actors, the director, the cinematographer and
camera/lighting crew, set directors, costumers, makeup
artists, location scouts and masters, the sound department,
editors – and the single most important talent: that of
gathering the money to pay for everyone else's creative work.

Complaint #12, Stated Another Way: "Respect The Writer's Vision."

It's a reverse pyramid. The actors (casting) and
directors attached to a project are often given
more importance than the writer, however...
without a script, actors and directors would have
no work. Audiences have been groomed to go see
a film based on it's cast and directors, but what
about marketing the writers as well so that
producers can bank on who wrote it as well.
Respect the writers vision. When one writer is
allowed to remain attached to their own project
and not have other writers do the re-writes or
take over, the project is often more cohesive and
welcomed by audiences as less "hollywood" or a
more engaging movie experience.

There are two ways for a writer to have his or her vision
"respected." The first is to be the one who puts up the quarter
of a million (microbudget) to $100 million or more for a
tentpole or blockbuster. Come up with the money, and believe
me, they'll give your vision all the respect in the world.

The second way to have your writer's vision respected is
to have a track record of making money for the people who do

143

risk that investment.

Do I seem to be confusing the terms, "respect" and "making money" in the comments above? Well, I'm not. "Respect" and "making money" (that is, successfully selling the product to audiences) may not seem to be the same thing to you, but in the entertainment business, they are.

Admittedly, that is a difficult idea to accept if you regard yourself as an artist painting with words. However, to succeed, the aspiring screenwriter must accept the fact that movies and TV are both collaborative media and very expensive to create, and that therefore, the visions which receive the highest respect are those of the person who gathers together the money and the people who make the final product ... if they make a profit on the movie or TV show, that is.

"Audiences Have Been Groomed" ... Not So

As to this notion that "Audiences have been groomed..."

Hogwash.

The author of the comment seems to be implying that audiences don't really know what they want, and that the industry has coaxed and duped a ticket-buying, subscription-buying, and advertising-watching pack of sheeple into accepting what the industry (for reasons not hinted at) wants to serve up.

However, what would it look like if the reverse were true, and that audiences have groomed the industry to serve up those entertainment products which audiences want? Why, it would look exactly like what we have: a business in which the biggest budgets go to star vehicles, remakes, toy tie-ins, comic-book-based superhero flicks, and tentpole movies.

This truth is obvious if you trouble yourself to examine what is actually produced, as opposed to that which is at the top of the box-office charts. As I discussed above, the industry makes a lot of movies and TV shows which are not star vehicles, remakes, toy tie-ins, or comic-book-based superhero flicks. These productions don't sell a lot of tickets. They end up in less visible markets. And spending money to advertise the screenwriter probably would not add a penny to the box office take or the bottom line.

Along the same vein, regarding the remark, "welcomed by audiences as less 'hollywood' or a more engaging movie experience":

I've put in a lot of time at auteur-based independent cinema over the years. And I've not failed to notice the obvious: that attendance is low and theater runs are short. I used to be a frequent customer of the marvelous little Beverly 13 theaters at the Beverly Center in Los Angeles. The fare served up by the Beverly 13 was eclectic and quirky, reflecting the individual artistic visions of writers and directors. Alas, that fare was not sufficiently "welcomed by audiences" or enough of "a more engaging movie experience" to keep the doors open. The Beverly 13 is long gone.

Complaint #13:
"Writers Should Be Paid As Much As Producers"

> "Writers should be paid more on par with producers, including points on the end. Without the script, there IS NO PRODUCTION."

Making apologies and seeking your forgiveness in advance ...

With the number of screenplays floating around town seeking the comfort of a producer's arms, "the script" could be replaced without great difficulty by another script, and a different movie could be made. So, without "the script," there IS a production. Just a different one.

Given how hungry film crews get, it is equally true that there would be no movie without the caterer. And given how eager everyone is to be paid, the bookkeeper is vital, too. That is, many people's contributions are vital to making a movie or TV show, and many very talented people compete constantly to land those jobs – just as you are competing with many other screenwriters to have your work selected as "the script" for production.

It is not the screenplay, but the collective creative work called "the movie" which is the work of art (or junk, or in most cases, something in between). The 1976 western, "The Missouri Breaks," for example, was shot with an incomplete script. Directed by the great Arthur Penn, with Brando and Nicholson ad-libbing some of their lines, it was trashed by critics at the time, but it is now regarded by many aficionados of Westerns as a classic.

Over the years, I've written daily newspaper news, business news, how-to books on tech and screenwriting subjects, speeches for U.S. senators, laws, U.S. Senate reports on laws, magazine articles, spec screenplays, marketing literature, and more. And I've never worked at or heard of a business or government office in which the writers made as much as the person who ran the show.

So please: exhibiting humility, rather than a big ego, before the gods and goddesses of entertainment is a valuable behavioral trait. If you believe that you and your screenplay are the very center of the Universe, go ahead and believe it, but it is in your best interest, diplomatically speaking, to hide that belief.

Complaint #14:
"The 'free option' should be outlawed and endless free rewrites should also be abolished."

> Unproduced writers like me tend to be either ignored or shat upon by production companies, studios, and the like. ... The concept of the "free option" should be outlawed...The concept of "endless free rewrites" should also be abolished.

Regarding the "free option," if the commenter means that a producer asks for an option without paying for it, I agree that this is difficult to accept. However, it's not going to be outlawed. You may even find some support for the "free option" among writers who are desperate enough to get in a producer's door to accept such a deal.

If I were still writing screenplays, I might accept an unpaid option for a first screenplay if the producer's credentials and plans impressed me enough.

Your choices on that are straightforward. You can say "No, thank you" and resume marketing that work. Or you can conclude that you're not likely to get a better offer soon for that work (or that you really don't want to spend the time and effort marketing it any more), and take that deal, then go to work on the next screenplay, in the hope of a better offer.

Regarding free rewrites, I think it depends on an array of factors, and I've made my argument on this above. If you make it into the Writers' Guild, you will be paid for rewrites, but only if the script is to be made under the auspices of one of the well-endowed signatories to the Writers Guild contract. That's because they can afford it, and the guild was able to negotiate that term in its contract with them. However, it covers relatively few of all purchased screenplays.

Complaint #15:
"Producers Insist That You Promote Yourself On Social Media" ... What?

> Producers put too much emphasis on a writer's social media presence. If a writer has a healthy presence on Facebook, Twitter or a blog site, I'm told that the producer is more apt to consider reading a script from that writer. Fine. But what if that script is very weak -- poor structure, limited or no character development, etc. What does the social media presence have to do with a scriptwriter's skills? I'd rather be spending my time writing scripts and improving my skills. Even Stephen King says in his non-fiction book, "On Writing," to get away from the TV and Internet and write. I agree. I'd like to see producers step away from this myth about social

media. Just because a writer can write a 141-character Tweet or amusing blog doesn't mean they can write a 110-page screenplay.

I don't know where this idea comes from about needing a social media presence. I have never heard that, and not one producer, agent, reader, contest executive, contest judge, teacher, or screenplay consultant contacted for this book said or hinted at any such thing. In fact, the only industry comments on social media for this survey were from two producers who said that pestering them on social media was in their lists of the worst possible behaviors by screenwriters. So my guess is that the writer of this comment is either misinformed or is speaking about an individual producer who is an outlier from the norm.

Also, I am not a fan of marketing one's screenplays on most social media. However, you might consider marketing on LinkedIn – if you do it right.

LinkedIn is not principally a "social" medium. It is there to make professional and business connections. Self-marketing on LinkedIn can be effective <u>if done right</u>. I'll go into that in my marketing book. Meanwhile, it's easy enough to figure out for yourself how to effectively use LinkedIn; just google the subject.

Complaint #16:
"You Should Retain Rights To Your Work" (?)

Aspiring screenwriters should be allowed to retain the rights to their work.

You <u>do</u> retain rights to your work, until such time as someone buys those rights. When you sell a screenplay, those rights are the very thing you sell. If the author of this comment means that the writer should be able to retain the rights after selling the screenplay, then I cannot imagine a circumstance in which a producer would agree to pay and then not own the rights to the screenplay.

Possibly the commenter is referring to situations like that of Amazon Studios, maybe? For those who don't know, when you submit to Amazon Studios, Amazon claims to own certain rights to the work, without compensating you. Under the rights claimed in its legal agreement, Amazon can distribute your work within its systems, and allow others to comment on or make revisions to it. The agreement does not give Amazon the right to make and distribute a movie from your script without a further agreement to pay you for the work. However, exactly how that subsequent step comes about, especially after others may have revised your screenplay in the Amazon system, is unclear to me. You can read Amazon's pack of legal agreements at:

https://studios.amazon.com/help/submission-agreement

Depending on the status of your screenwriting career and the quality of the script, this Amazon Studios arrangement might work for you. You get feedback, collaboration (which some people love, and others hate), and a chance at production (and being paid) in exchange for Amazon claiming to own certain rights to the screenplay. It is one approach to getting a screenplay produced.

Complaint #17:
"Better Connections Are Needed" ...Or Better Grammar, Maybe?

> I won a third party sponsorship for my first project. However, after that because I am not known the door's have not opened to me yet. It appears its who you know not how talented you are.
>
> It's a closed nit group.

I know it's is unkind of me to point this out, but in the mere three sentences in the first comment, I counted six grammatical errors. If you wrote that comment, and your screenwriting is similarly challenged grammatically, are you sure that the obstacle is lack of connections, and not your writing?

The industry is unforgiving about poor grammar. There is the distinct possibility that if you are sending work out with a lot of grammatical fractures, you <u>are</u> known: you're known as someone who writes badly.

Regarding the second comment: Ouch! The correct phrase is "close-knit," and the industry is indeed a closed, nit-picking group when it comes to language like your sentence. This commenter might consider sending a recent script to a screenplay proofreader to see how many corrections are made.

Complaint #18:
Working Writer: "Too Many Notes, Conflicting Notes, Irrelevant Notes"

> "Being bombarded with a ton of notes, especially if they're unclear... working from their notes are fine, but I've definitely (and am currently) dealt with producers who give a ton of notes, every idea that pops into their heads, even if those ideas don't pertain to the story, could be a whole separate movie, etc... So 'unfocused notes.'"

So true, so true. Most aspiring writers have no idea what they're in for when they finally sell something, and are "lucky" (?) enough to be kept on to do the rewriting, rather than have the script handed over to a script rewriter.

Some notes are indeed off-topic or dumber than a box of hair. However...

Here's what two professional screenwriter friends of mine say about dealing with notes: Don't argue. Deal with the notes to the best of your ability. In your next meeting, be prepared to discuss what you've done in response to their input. Even if you've done something completely different from that which they've suggested, they should appreciate that you have tried to heed their notes.

Complaint(s) #19:
Real-Life Horror Stories About Producers

"I had a $20,000 contract negated because the producers wanted to tell a different true story (more sleazy) than the one I had pitched and they approved. More honesty up front - if possible!"

"I sold a 30 page treatment to NBC, then they said we'll hire a writer to write teleplay (I guess the treatment wrote itself). The writer turned in the teleplay and they asked where is the "great scene about . . . " The writer responded we didn't need it. That went on for about thirty minutes. The writer missed the entire point of the story and turned it into mush. NBC then decided not to produce the picture. It went into turn around. CBS picked it up. They brought in a writer (three actually) paid them and rejected two of the teleplays, accepted one and the movie was produced. Both networks spent thousands of dollars on writers but wouldn't give me, the original writer, a shot at writing the teleplay. Dumb, dumb, dumb."

There may have been details and circumstances not revealed in the comments above, but as a general principle, one can certainly understand and sympathize with the frustrations of these two writers.

To the author of the first comment, and others who have had similar experiences: Yes, it is painful to see your creation changed, and especially to see it cheapened.

Very likely, more than once in your screenwriting career, you will face the choice of submitting to the will of the producer and changing your screenplay, or if you haven't signed the deal yet, declining to do so and seeking another buyer.

However, once you have sold the rights, then that producer owns it and has the right to impose his or her vision on it. It's frustrating to see one's work sleazed down, but it's their right to do so. That can be hard to accept.

Regarding the second comment: Yes, given that it was your story (absent other considerations not mentioned), probably both NBC and CBS should have had you write the first draft, receive notes, and write a second. Judging from the facts presented, the networks had nothing to lose by letting you do the writing and a rewrite before thinking about taking it away.

However, the devil is often in the details and in circumstances not revealed. For example, was there a personality clash? Was it an incompetent producer or studio executive? Or did you signal somehow by your behavior that you thought he/she was not competent? Had the first producer promised work to another writer? Did the producers see you as being too inexperienced? Did you and the producers or execs differ on how the story should be written (which seems likely from the anecdote)? Was it something else?

If you had differences over the story, or if they had the perception (valid or not) that you were insufficiently experienced, or if you gave them the idea that you "knew" you were the brightest person in the room and they weren't, then this result is the sort of fact of Hollywood life which new writers have to get used to. The original writer of a screenplay or treatment often has it taken away for a rewrite by someone else.

I suggest that you congratulate yourself for selling the story, use that story credit in your resume, and focus on your next script.

Positive Experiences:

"I haven't been treated unfairly or poorly by any of the production companies I've had my screenplays sent to."

"I met my first and only producer via a
Screenwriter's Festival a few years ago where he
really liked an idea I pitched in an open pitching
competition the Festival hosts. It was at the
networking drinks where we spoke briefly and he
approached me! It was an amazing feeling. Fast
forward to present day, I have written a script in
which I wanted to send out to this producer for
him to read and if possible get some feedback.
Not only did he read it and gave feedback, he did
this twice on two separate drafts! I can proudly
say that this experience with a producer is
brilliant and shows that in fact producers are
interested in finding new talent and great scripts
alongside from professional A-List writers. I can
only dream to have the same experience with
producers to come. I can only imagine that this
producer read my script in his free time as it
wasn't something the production companies he
works for would produce. That means something
and I can't thank him enough for doing that.
Producers must be under extreme conditions to
channel their efforts and time to projects that a)
fit within what they're looking for and b) make
money."

"I think producers as a group do a pretty good
job. This is a crazy industry and producers are in
the cross hairs more than anyone else. A lot of
the crazy isn't them, personally - though some
are better than others. The best ones understand
what makes a script work, the worst ones don't.
Even if the bad ones would just read Save The
Cat it would make life easier and make
discussions more productive."

I don't think there's anything wrong with the way
production companies treat aspiring writers.
They're simply going about their business, and

often aspiring writers don't understand enough about how the industry works and so they make nuisances of themselves. As for professional writers, I do think the standard needs to be changed such that production companies more regularly pay for work, rather than getting so much for free. But I guess it's a buyer's market.

11: Writers' Complaints About Agents

Write Screenplay, Get Agent? Not Likely

This chapter recites and discusses the complaints of respondents to the screenwriter survey about producers and production companies. My thoughts can be found at the bottom of this chapter.

The question was:

> ABOUT AGENTS: What's wrong with the way agents and agencies, or a particular agent or agency, treat aspiring screenwriters, or have treated you, and what could and should they do differently? NOTE: We are not going to publish the name(s) of any agents or agencies in this e-book. However, if you wish to name a particular organization, feel free to do so.

The responses, positive comments first:

The positive comments...all three of them:

> I've had four different agents in my career and they have all treated me very well.

> Nothing [is wrong with agents]. Agents are just doing their jobs. It's in the aspiring writer's interest to figure out how to navigate the system, but it's not the agent's job to teach aspirants how to do so.

> Haven't had a bad experience yet

The negative comments:

> It is difficult to access [agents] if you have an original idea. They just play it safe.

Working as a script reader for one of them made me soon realize that nothing positive can be expected, unless one wants to become an agent too.

I'm an older writer (70 yrs old) and agents may not see a future earning potential in a relationship.

Only money. Don't allow access to artists who might work without money.

I don't think there are enough agents, or at least good agents in business for the number of writers there are. I also don't think they take a writer seriously, unless that person has been published. They should be willing to take more writers under their wing and assist with mentoring them, as well as letting them know what type of scripts producers are looking for...

My current manager put out a few weak attempts at furthering my career. After there were no nibbles, I was quickly forgotten.

Sometimes my agent seemed to show preference towards other clients. I was not very needy, but do like to feel appreciated.

Hard to get in front of.

[Name deleted] from [agency name deleted] was the last agent I had. Her behavior and the manner in which she interacted with me imply to me that she is a stone cold sociopath. Although she did initially get me some work, after the opportunities dwindled, she started asking me for money. Sucker that I am, I often paid her phone bill, her vet bill, and paid her debts to others. I had to get a day job to support myself, so she did not hesitate to ask for money from me. Every time she asked, she told me that we were so close to getting a big pay day to fund the studio she wanted to build. She even went as far as writing up several contracts for my spec scripts in which she had offered to pay me $100K per script, plus producer's fees and a whole bunch of other nonsense. My belief in her lies almost rendered me homeless...

Difficult to get their attention with good writing - has to be something else - winning an award, graduating from a good school, etc.

Agents I've sent work to have either explained they already represent enough clients or do not appreciate the material sent them.

I was lied to and led down the primrose path by a leading agent at one of the biggest agencies if the town for a year, and asked to keep my sought after script off the market, contests and out of any other's hands for almost a year, and then I was ignored, forgotten and treated shoddily after all sorts of overtures ... Highly unprofessional, unethical and just plain shitty treatment.

Most agents don't seem to want to take on new clients unless a screenplay has already been sold.

Self-centered.

Not being proactive sometimes in getting your info out there. They should be paid only on what they do not on any other material you send out that they had no hand in getting out there.

It is the writer's job to impress the agent. again,

some agents are age prejudice. I try to find an agent and develop a relationship with that agent, and I make sure what I send presents a professional endeavor. If your agent isn't working for you... ask why.

Never hearing back.

I had an epic work show up on screen based upon the: a) subject b) suggested budget c) Lead actor So, no more agency/agent queries or interviews without the appropriate legal security for me!

The agents I've met were more concerned with my pitch than my writing. Since I am concerned with trying to write a good screenplay, first and foremost, I look for guidance and feedback I can use to improve. I wrote four screenplays and got frustrated, stopped...There's only so much rejection I can handle.

Most agents don't take the time to even address an aspiring screenwriter, especially those of color. And if you are over 18 as a writer, you are over the hill. Not everyone enjoys slapstick comedy, adults go to the movies too and I mean those of us past 35.

Difficult to get access to agents.

Agents and managers follow suit to the obsession of production companies. They scan available material for what can be immediately sold and do not see it as one of their objectives to develop good idea into sellable scripts/presentations.

The agent I had never got anyone to read my screenplay.

Unless one is recommended you stand very little chance of getting your script read.

Since the agent's goal is to make money (not careers), it is only logical that they focus on known talent. The trouble is how does one become known in order to be focused upon? The old Catch 22. Hip-pocketing can work, but the struggling screenwriter will be dropped before the morning coffee arrives if they do not perform. Personally, most agents I have meet are friendly and interested in meeting new writers.

Note on "hip pocketing":

"It means the agent will submit your work for you if you need to make a submission, but you do not have a contract with the agency and you are not on the official roster of represented clients." – **This according to GirlinGray on the Done Deal pro message board.** In real life, her name is Max Adams, author of The Screenwriter's Survival Guide and The New Screenwriter's Survival Guide. Great books to read. See:

http://www.screenwriterssurvivalguide.com/

http://www.amazon.com/Screenwriters-Survival-Guerrilla-Meeting-Tactics-ebook/dp/B00AK0LYJG and see a bit more about her book in the chapter on self-marketing.

Maybe try opening a few more doors and at least take a look at some (Fresh) new work.

They try to do a good job, but within time constraints they are only human and can devote their time to those that are making money.

More agents, managers, & producers should be open to reading unproduced writers.

I've found it very difficult to even get an agent to

read one of my scripts. I've found producers to be more open to reading scripts from uncredited writers.

...promising to read when met at a party, and never getting back to me at all.

A better question is what is right with agents and agencies. No one wants to read or respond to query letters, period! ... Agents only want to entertain writers who have a track record of sales. I completely understand this because it is a complete waste of time and money for agents to evaluate which writer is worthy of the current market... Agents do not want writers who write, they want writers who write MTV style: few words, no dialogue, no description. It is completely disheartening. Yet very connected writers are selling. It may be complete crap, and go nowhere, but it at least provides flash-in-the-pan income. I was advised by an agent on a MOV that was in pre-production at CBS, a dozen years ago, to simplify it to the most basic word structure. I flatly refused. She dumped me.

I sometimes think that it is not what you know but who you know, and agents are hesitant to represent someone with few connections.

They should promote more young aspiring writers, female writers or screenwriters of color.

Read more than just the treatment.

They want to sell there own nonsense.

[I have] not bothered with agents

If you don't have any credits they get put out if

you bother them.

They act like they do something special once you get in with them, at the end of the day once you get signed they ignore you till you book something.

They make it hard on purpose.

I haven't had much interaction with Agents because in my humble opinion, I don't think it's really necessary to have an Agent in reality. Production companies shut down aspiring writers to read their unsolicited work, however agents, the majority of the time, won't both with aspiring writers because they don't have credits etc. I've had 2 encounters with Agents: 1 via email and 1 via pitching at a Festival. The via email was quite sarcastic towards me. I originally asked a client of hers a question, however being unable to answer said to email his agent. Her reply was quite instantaneous and rather insulting and patronising. Not good. The other whom I pitched at I caught up later at a networking drinks event afterwards. Rather drunk, he shut me down saying that 'Writers with no produced work should never pitch at an Agent.' Also not good. I don't see why there is any need of Agents. I would rather prefer the Manager route as that's all about coaching and mentoring viable aspiring writers with potential. They give back something to the writer, which I deem worth their cut of the credit.

No publishing offer, no agent.

I've been disappointed at promises not kept. Specifically, an agent who spoke at an AFF roundtable and said she would 'guarantee one read' for each of the six scriptwriters present, but then did not follow through.

There just isn't enough time for agents to nurture aspiring writers. It's about the bottom line, not the craft. But without the support of an entire community, agents included, how can an aspiring writer afford to write and write well. They must be given the time and attention and money to hone and perfect their craft and find their voice.

Most agents I've contacted like my work, but want to sign me after I've already done the deal. Then they want to climb on board for their cut.

Agents are there to cut deals. If a writer expects more he's just fooling himself. I don't know about other writers, but I've got thick skin. I wish they'd be more honest - to the point of blunt.

Agents and Managers are the same. They don't want to look at anything new or different.

Not willing or able to consider the material from new writers.

I just had a recent experience that was rather annoying. I had an agent that took interest and raved about the first sample I sent them, but when I sent them a second sample they didn't seem too fond of it and suddenly back-peddled a bit on the first one. It would have made more sense if they simple said they didn't like the second one. But, I also sent them pitch packets with the scripts which leads me to believe they only read those and not the scripts. It's hard to say because it was like dealing with a Jekyll and Hyde.

Literary agents listed for my area in directories are no longer in business. I would like to see more up to date listings for agents, at least, in my area.

Landing an agent is about as difficult as signing with a production company.

Agents are hard to identify or get, but they are definitely more available than producers

My understanding is that agents want little to do with a writer until the writer has proven themselves. Can't really argue with that.

Agents and agencies are not built to take chances. Therefore, if you do not have a proven track record already, they don't want to take the chance on taking you on as a client. The first question I have been asked so many times is - 'How many scripts have you sold?'

Agents are a problem because its preference. The films made to day are horrible but what agent signed the writer. I feel it's too much bias behavior.

Need to be awareness about how to communication with deaf writers or any disabilities.

My Observations About Agents And The Comments Above

1. Seeking An Agent Is Usually A Waste of Your Time

The responses of writers regarding agents do indeed reflect the facts as they are. Agents, on the whole, are indifferent to new, unsold, unproduced screenwriters. That indifference is nearly universal. It is probably not worth your time and effort to seek an agent unless you have a sale to a producer pending, and need an agent to negotiate the deal, or maybe if you have just won a contest or two, or you have some other special credentials.

Why can't you land an agent? Why are they so inaccessible?

First, there aren't enough agents to go around. By far.

Second, they are businesspeople with bills to pay and clients to serve. They have a pretty good idea of what they need to do to make money, and only so many hours in the day to do it.

Third, serving as an agent to a new, unproduced, unknown screenwriter is a money-losing, time-wasting proposition for them 98 percent of the time. Even if the relationship does end up being beneficial to the agent, that break-even date is usually years later with a new, breaking-in client.

You can waste your own time blaming agents for this state of affairs, or you can accept reality as it is, and use other means to give yourself a chance of success.

"But without the support of an entire community, agents included, how can an aspiring writer afford to write and write well?"

The short answer:

1. Once again, no one asked you to write screenplays, so why do you feel entitled to be supported?

2. There is a lot of support out there anyway; you just need to find it. But it's extremely unlikely that you will find it from agents.

3. Others afford it, so why not you? Structure your life to make time to write. Look up Emily Nussbaum's article on Kenya Barris, and post it at the entrance to your pity party.

4. Yes, it's hard. I know. I made a bit of progress, winning

some contests, and then I spent years at it, and then I ultimately gave up.   Working at it was a good life decision at the time; so was quitting when I quit. I blame no one. Not them, not myself.

5. Go ahead and whine about it all you want to friends (and to me anonymously in your survey responses). Venting complaints now and then is good for morale. But never complain to the industry. They don't want to hear it, and it will hurt you professionally.

1a. Here Are Two Points Of View From Knowledgeable People Who Somewhat Disagree With My Comments Above:

Producer-writer Chad Gervich, the author of a helpful insider's book, <u>How To Manage Your Agent: A Writer's Guide To Hollywood Representation</u>, has written that yes, it's possible to land an agent, but low expectations are in order. Two important points he makes are that (a) agents make most of their money by staffing TV shows, not by selling feature scripts; and (b) that "baby" writers (that is, newcomers) typically don't make money for the agent for years. See this web page for his views and information on his book:

https://goodinaroom.com/blog/get-literary-agent/

One of the free introductory telephone courses offered now and then by Hal Croasmun of ScreenwritingU.com is "How To Get An Agent."

This chapter doesn't dispute what either of them has to say about how to go about it. However, as Chad Gervich points out, thousands of writers are seeking agents every day (usually for feature scripts), while the industry has about 200 job openings for staff writers on TV shows, and agents have far less interest in taking on unknown, unproduced feature writers.

So your odds are long if you're aiming to write for TV, and far longer if you're seeking an agent for a feature. My opinion on how to go about marketing is...

2. Do Your Own Marketing And/Or Pay For Help

"...want to sign me after I've already done the deal. <u>Then they want to climb on board for their cut</u>."

The short version of my answer to this comment is:

1. I hear this all the time. Again, I suggest that most aspiring writers should stop thinking of an agent as your principal marketer.

2. However, the view that they "climb on board for their cut" leaps out of the page at me as a self-destructive attitude, for two reasons:

First, it seems to imply that the author of this comment thinks an agent doesn't provide value in ways other than marketing. Unless you have an entertainment industry attorney (or are one), this is dangerously naive thinking.

You need an agent or an entertainment-industry lawyer to negotiate your deal. If you have a deal pending, seek out one or the other. A lawyer typically works for an hourly rate, but might work for a percentage. An agent works for ten percent. It's your choice, but a variation on the old saying, "A man who is his own lawyer has a fool for a client" applies here.

Second. consider the fact that about a hundred thousand writers are out there seeking representation from just a few hundred agents. If you land one, that agent will want to sell more of your work and find you modestly high-paying work as a new TV-show writer, with the possibility of a six- or seven-figure income down the road. And you're going to resent that person? Doesn't that seem just a wee bit shortsighted? To me, it doesn't seem merely shortsighted. It seems like one of the fundamental reasons many aspiring writers need this book.

Thankfully, "Write script, get an agent" is not the only marketing plan or approach available to you as an aspiring screenwriter. In fact, it's far from the best these days. In further fact, it's probably the worst marketing plan because it rarely works unless you have special credentials or a deal pending, or have been focusing on writing for TV, with a lot of great sample pilot scripts. All that time and effort* you spend seeking an agent could be spent marketing yourself.

*I'm in much the same position as you and your screenplay are with regard to this book. All the time I've spent researching and writing it will be wasted if I don't spend more time and effort marketing it than I'm spending on its creation.

> Let me repeat that, because it is true for you as well as for me: <u>If I want this book to sell, I will spend more time and effort marketing it and managing the business of marketing it than the substantial amount of time and effort I have put into creating it.</u>

The key difference between you, aspiring screenwriter, and me in this regard is that I knew before I started the research that I would be my own marketer (and dealmaker), and I know how, because I have 20+ years' experience as a publisher, running the business end of writing.

My View: As Marketers, Agents Are Largely Yesterday's News For Aspiring Feature Writers

In my view, as marketers of feature screenplays for newcomers, agents are an anachronism. Their value as the principal marketers of screenplays is left over from the days:

● before email and fax marketing

● before certain professional social media existed (LinkedIn, for example)

● before database marketing, mass mailings, and email blasting could be done from your personal computer

● before you could make a web-based show to display your own work (which used to require a $16,000-and-up movie camera, but which you can nowadays shoot in high resolution on your cell phone)

167

● before there were so many markets for screenplays that no single agent can possibly have working relationships with every producer

● before you could put a trailer or an entire web series online

● before you had a cell phone to rapidly dial a lot of people in a row

● before Inktip and Scriptblaster and Smartgirls Productions and the many script consultants with industry connections who will forward work they deem to be meritorious to their industry contacts

● before all the other ways new writers have of gaining attention for screenplays such as the many contests with ties to the industry, live and online pitch events, script listing services, and online directories of producer contact information

● before the Blacklist and less formal groups like it were around to circulate great scripts without writers knowing who was reading them.

In other words, today you have vastly more ways to market yourself and your work effectively and efficiently than were available back when agents were the vital marketing link to the industry for the unproduced, unknown screenwriter.

So take charge of your own marketing. Value agents for their dealmaking skills and for their contacts once you have established yourself with a sale or two.

And feel blessed if an agent "climbs on for her or his cut."

12: Writers' Complaints About Screenplay Contests

Nothing Gets Writers Worked Up Like Paying To Be Rejected

This chapter recites and comments on the complaints of respondents to the screenwriter survey about screenplay contests. Most of my comments are at the end.

The question was:

> ABOUT SCREENPLAY CONTESTS: What's wrong with the way a particular screenplay contest, or contests generally, treat aspiring screenwriters, or have treated you, and what could and should they do differently?

Most Answers Were Highly Negative

Most of the commentary was negative. Extremely so. Most likely, this extreme negativity reflects these realities:

● The average contest doesn't make enough money* to invest heavily in the careers of winners. So the marketing of winners' scripts is typically not very thorough.

● The odds of winning any contest are low, numerically speaking.

● Many screenwriters have an unrealistic expectation that "win contest" automatically translates to "industry buys my script," without much effort by the writer in between. It rarely works that way. Even the prestigious Motion Picture Academy's Nicholl Fellowships had only 17 movies produced from winning scripts between 1982 and 2013, according to a Wikipedia article, although it's fair to assume that quite a few more than 17 were sold.

* It is a widely held misconception among screenwriters that the typical screenplay contest makes fat profits. This is reflected in the comments below. This is far from true for most

contests. More on this below.

The Positive Comments About Contests:

"Yes, They Are Worthwhile":

> I have entered dozens of contests, with shorts
> and full length, and comments are often brutal,
> but true! When I finally "got it" in terms of what
> a screenplay is supposed to be, then I won some
> awards. It took me ten years to "get it." NO
> complaints. When I first started out writing, my
> first book was Screenwriting by Richard Walter,
> and he said it would take ten years and I said
> "shit, really?" but he was absolutely correct!

> I have had positive experience with contests. I
> have placed and even won some. As long as the
> contest keeps everyone informed as to status - I
> am fine with that. The ones where you apply and
> pay a fee and never hear from again are suspect.

> Nothing is wrong with how screenplay contests
> treat writers. It's up to the writer to do their
> research on which contests they want to submit
> to, and do the extra leg work into finding out
> how the contests treats writers, their readers, etc.

> There should be more of them and fewer
> restrictions on getting it into the contest or types
> of stories to tell.

> My limited experience is with Sundance, and
> they were terrific. I wrote a script that made the
> first cut of their director's program, and they
> provided excellent feedback for why it was
> eventually rejected. I really appreciated it.

> I have won two competitions and have been

treated great. No real world results from them, but it is just a matter of writing the right thing for the right time.

I think that the contests seem to be fair. If you are a budding screenwriter, I think you need more information in order to participate.

I am happy with this so far. I entered a contest in 2010 with two scripts, one of which was long-listed; the other short-listed. Comments were most encouraging.

I have been treated well with every submission.

Screenplay contests are a matter of opinion, what one person may like another doesn't.

I've had no issues with contests I have entered.

Haven't had a bad experience yet

Only entered one contest and had good experience...maybe because I was a finalist. Hard to determine how valuable any particular contest is for the writer. Not clear how much credibility producers put on certain contests.

The Negative Comments:

"Scams/Money-Making Gimmicks/Too Expensive"

I believe they're scams. I laugh when I receive the list of winners and see numerous scripts. Are they all that good? And have any ever really been produced? Consider the number of scripts that any given contest receives. Perhaps 2,000 scripts? Now multiply that by an average entry fee of $40. That's $80,000. Give $1,000 to the

<u>top winner and some money to script readers.
The individual running the contest just made
about $70,000. Not bad.</u>*

*Author's note: the comment above is obviously sincere.
It is also revealing about attitudes and beliefs versus reality.
The part I underlined is far from the truth, in my experience as
a contest executive. This comment and others on this theme
prompted me to add at the end of this chapter a table showing
the composite four-year average income and expenses of an
actual screenwriting contest I co-owned and ran.

I feel quite safe in concluding from my experience that
the average contest doesn't get anywhere near 2,000 entries. A
few hundred to maybe a thousand is typical.

The contest I ran was one of the bigger ones in the
industry at the time, when there were fewer contests. It offered
multiple prizes, a top prize of $5,000, and feedback on all
scripts entered, and it advertised winning and high-placing
scripts to about 300 industry contacts.

Also, it was able to advertise more widely that most
contests because we published one of the two international
screenwriting print magazines, and enjoyed the status and
full-page advertising space which came with it. We advertised
the contest repeatedly to our email blast list of 120,000
screenwriters. We also advertised through Withoutabox and
with ads placed with various other media (Moviebytes, Done
Deal, software partners, and more).

In other words, our prizes were strong, and our
marketing and advertising were much broader than most
contests could afford.

However, that contest still averaged only about 1,450
entries a year, not 2,000. Again, this was at a time when there
were far fewer competing contests. See the composite budget
below.

**"Scams/Money-Making Gimmicks/Not Worth The
Money," Continued...**

Too many contests gaining access fee which makes a very lucrative business.

Sorry, I stopped wasting time with contests long ago. Why send contest fees to people who are just trying to make a living from the mass of daydreaming screenwriters? Even the ones who run free contests end up acting quite carelessly. When they make mistakes and mishandle the contact addresses they have to deal with, they don't think for one second about the consequences on the screenwriters' lives they messed up with. The good people at the BBC Writersroom can leave you heartbroken after making you hope for nothing.

Contests that charge a fee to enter are scams & I have never, nor would I ever, enter one. Aside from actors, screenwriters are the cash-poorest caste in Hollywood.

Too expensive, money making gimmick, should always include feedback

Never entered competitions because of entry fees and proximity from Nigeria.

I've learned over the years that maybe a dozen or so screenplay contests will really get you anywhere. The other ones aren't really recognized, but it's like volunteer work, it looks good on your resume, or query letter to state you've won a contest. All of them should offer feedback on your screenplay, so we know it was actually read, and that feedback should be specific, for example, on page 15, this happens when it should indicate it is CLEARLY the protagonist's choice, etc. Some of the feedback, I've gotten is so generalized, you are not sure what they've meant or how to fix your script. They should have larger cash prizes through sponsors, or at least ensure an option, or have it produced. If it's a winning script, why wouldn't some company who produces that type of work/genre not want to produce it?

Most contests just seem like money-making ventures and don't offer any real benefits to screenwriters.

Screenwriting contests are either too expensive to enter or offer little potential of introducing writers to production facilitators.

I think they look "sexy" and slick, and great if you place or win, but are in fact just money makers for the organization. Wish there were more categories. and more winners... Though, I have dabbled in sending my work this year to a few just to see how it transpires.

They seem to be more geared towards profit rather than the writer.

Many screenplay contests seem to be out there only to make money. I have been winner, finalist and on the second place for half a dozen times now and never got a call from anybody who would be interested in my work. All you get is a mail where you are offered to buy a statue or a certificate.

I entered a contest or two, and got zero feedback. It's like they don't even read your script. They just take the money and run.

They are very expensive and I don't see the point. Every time I submit my script to a producer or agent it's the same thing except all it costs me is postage.

Too many screenplay contests are cash-grabs that take advantage of hopeful wannabe writers.

Screenplay contests are another money grab. If an emerging writer wanted to submit a script to the top 10 or 15 contests, it would cost them a small fortune. Writers are paying these organizations when they often can't afford it and the meagre stipend they get on the off chance their script is chosen doesn't compensate them. This industry is more about who you know and even if you've written a great script, the chances of getting it produced are so few. Directors don't have to compete to win a job directing a project, actors don't have to send in audition tapes to a competition in order to show their talent, why make writers go through this farce? Amateur athletes seem to be the only other profession that competes for a prize and even they get corporate or community sponsorships.

Usually not worth the entry fee.

They are a money making scheme. I've done very well in the big ones, Nicholl's Fellowship for example. The rest are just to make money.

The entry fees are sometimes much too high compared to the benefits.

"Not Much Help/No Help Promoting Screenwriting Career"

Screenplay contests, as I have seen them (excluding Nicholl), do not further the career of most screenwriters. If they are stand-alone (not affiliated with a film festival), you have no idea what is happening with your script. There is better exposure in a film festival, where at least you may end up on the program. As a rule, I avoid them.

I have never entered a screenplay contest, and. to be honest, I am so dubious as to success in the industry, if entered.

I don't find much benefit in them.

I am very sceptical, there are so many, and they promise much, but I do not know of anyone who's career has been launched this way.

I never submit to contests because in general I feel they're expensive with very low odds of any success. Better off targeting producers specifically interested in your type of work.

I have not found contests to be much help getting onto the business.

"Want More/Better Feedback"

Need more feedback

Should give more feedback

I wish I could get feedback (or the option to ask for feedback).

"Contest Judges Are Amateurs/Too Young/Untrained Etc."

Many of the readers are not writers. Many of them are too young to know anything, about life, scripts, movies or anything else. And too many don't read anything but scripts. And they follow what a screenwriting book tells them to comment on. It's often a bit too much by rote or by amateurs. Yet, they take your money and scripts and hand them to those utterly unqualified.

They are not transparent about the skills or professional backgrounds of their readers, or whether their readers are paid. The prices are high enough to suggest this is a purely for-profit venture. And often the prizes are not worth the effort or fees.

Some Screenplay contests are very subjective and the writer is many times judged by people who are not professionals or qualified to judge a screenplay contest. I have also found many contests to be nothing more than a money making scam... There should be a way for the Industry to vet screenplay contests and come up with an approved list.

The big question is who are the judges for any screenwriting contest and what qualifications do they have? Aside the major ones, (Nicholl, etc.), most seem to in the business of separating aspiring screenwriters from their hard-earned money.

"I Fear That My Work Will Be Stolen"

I guess my concern with contests is the security of my submitted work.

I don't submit to screenplay contests for fear of plagiary

Don't make it clear the copyrights that are lost.

Other Complaints:

It's important to know that the contest is actually connecting you directly to producers and they are named. It's also important to know that your material is not being misused by other writers it would be useful to know who is actually reading and evaluating the material early on in the contest. Generally there is a lack of transparency around number of contestants in each category. Prizes are sometimes not as rewarding as they should be compared to the entry fee. Judges are often men there are very few women involved. Genres are incorrectly grouped together eg horror/thriller.

New writers are generally up against older experienced writers who know the in's and out of writing for contest organizers.

They do not reveal to you the distance your submission reached in their process of selecting winners.

Some. Contests are complications sometimes. And not friendly to disabilities.

Some contest do this but many don't, and that is specialize. I think horror scripts should be compared to horror scripts and love stories to love stories etc... I also think the contest judges should be familiar with the genre they are reading. If a judge has know idea how a Thriller works then he should not be reading a Thriller script.

Most contests are half baked and only seem to want to collect fees. Free ones such as BBC recently have rules such as only living in UK to be considered to be read.

I've done well in competition even though I have yet to win. I'm not a fan of contests due to the untrustworthy practices.

We need more notification. Some of us may not be as far along with our screenplay and need more time to prepare it.

I would appreciate more regular updates from contests, at least letting people know how many entries have been received. It keeps things in perspective.

I have tried three and did not even get an honorable mention. I did get approached about signing up for their courses or email blasts or newsletter, et.

There should be more contests that specialize in screenwriters of color, female writers and student writers.

I teach screenwriting at Columbia College Chicago. Entering contests are always recommended as a way to break into the business, but I think the odds of winning, even with a great screenplay, are so minimal, I wonder why no one suggests writing a play that, all things considered, might get produced, reviewed, and you can learn a lot from the experience. Plus, it's a bona fide writing credit that could potentially gain favor with a producer or agent.

I have seen and read that Contests may be biased towards certain writer's whom the readers, judges may be already familiar with. That's my only criticism.

I don't trust them.

Too many contests are bullshit. We had one in
Reno recently, and it was a joke.

Screenplay contests are a great sop while I work
to get good enough to sell.

I don't know if fellowships fall under this
heading, but I am feeling more and more they
are based on how many times you have applied
and who you know when it should be about the
work.

I enter them rarely. It seems that while a win in
one of those might be a feather in one's writing
scalp, most of the winning screenplays I've read I
wouldn't want to see on the screen. What's the
point?

Promise a lot but a lot of times it's more words
and promises than actual delivering what they
say.

My Take On Screenplay Contests

Disclosures:

1. I used to write spec screenplays. I entered my first
three screenplay contests principally because they offered cash
prizes, and I needed the money while I was in film school. As
mentioned elsewhere in this book, I won all three.

2. Then, I entered two contests which were both much
bigger in terms of numbers of entrants and more prestigious
(the Nicholl Fellowships and a Disney TV series competition).
I won nothing and heard nothing back. Because I had won
three less competitive contests, and because the synopsis I
submitted to Disney was quite brilliant (in my sole,
unqualified opinion at the time), I was outraged. I felt, most
deeply and very angrily, that I had been robbed and that the

Disney and Nicholl contests must have been rigged.

In fact, to this day, I still believe that the somewhere within, or around the edges of, the idea I submitted to Disney lies a great, memorable TV series.

They weren't rigged, of course, but my screenwriter's ego was so puffy and fragile at the time that making disparaging assumptions about these contests was a way to patch the leaks in my self-esteem. I've come to realize as I've matured that my synopsis was quite inadequate to evoke the mixed-genre subject matter. However, I couldn't see that then.

In other words, I was just like many of you who commented above: a disparager of screenplay contests. A believer that they were scams, rigged, et cetera.

3. Then, from 2007 through 2011, I was the chief executive of a publishing company which ran 11 screenwriting contests, five scene-writing contests, and two logline contests during that time. I participated in managing all of them, and even served as a contest judge.

That is to say, I have a good bit of experience with screenplay contests from all sides – as a winner, as a loser who believed I'd been scammed, as a contest manager, and as a contest judge. I even invented two contests.

It is obvious from the majority of comments above that screenplay contests are a great source of pain for aspiring screenwriters. To summarize the main complaints:

● They're accused of being scams.

● They're accused of making fat profits off financially strapped screenwriters.

● Judges are accused of being incompetent.

● Winning doesn't get a script sold.

● Some contests don't provide feedback.

● Others provide minimal feedback, but entrants want in-depth feedback.

181

● The feedback on "my brilliant screenplay" is "obviously wrong."

Are These Beliefs Mostly True or Mostly False?

Is there any truth at all to these accusations? Certainly some. In my view, the widely-held caustic view of screenplay contests arises from:

● The obvious, deep, and real pain and frustration of losing;

● Receiving nothing from some contests for the entry fee, or receiving only a brief, cryptic comment on the script, or – far worse for some writers – receiving a comment which is precisely to the point, but which the writer's ego can't take;

● The very common, very human inability to accept, after doing all that work, that one's work is deemed deficient, and worse, that it is so deemed by some invisible person who can't even be confronted (and who, therefore, must be "incompetent");

● The hope that placing in or winning a contest will, <u>in and of itself</u>, cause agents and producers to flock to oneself and bring about a sale.

Discussion Of These Points

As one writer notes above, being rejected by a producer costs only the price of sending the query letter, but you pay a contest (as much as $85) to receive only a rejection, or a rejection plus painful comments about your hard work. In my view, that fact is the single biggest reason screenplay contests receive much harsher treatment than producers and even agents from aspiring screenwriters: you pay good money for two kinds of emotional abuse.

Yes, it hurts deeply to enter contests and receive nothing but anonymous rejection for your time, effort, and emotional investment. I've been there, done that, and bought the T-shirt.

Uttering and retweeting conspiracy theories about

"scams" and "profiteering" and "incompetent" judges might offer some temporary comfort (and the "scam" accusation might be true about a small minority of lesser contests). However, this conspiracy-theory yakking is counterproductive in the long run. It wounds the soul and saps morale. It impedes the careers of those who foment it. Buying into such theories is wallowing in excuses rather than making progress.

Many of the comments also reflect the widespread, mistaken view that if you win a contest, it does most of your marketing for you.

The Truth, As I See It:

First, the raw numbers are stacked against you. Take the example from above of the hypothetical contest which gets (an unrealistically high) 2,000 entries at $40. If 20 screenplays "place" in that contest (quarterfinals and above), then, based purely on the numbers, your entry has one chance in a hundred of winning even the lowest level of recognition, and one chance in two thousand, numerically speaking, of winning the top prize.

That's depressingly low -- half as good as the odds of winning the New York Mafia numbers lottery. Also, consider this: Maybe your screenplay did merit "placing" in that contest, but it happened to be the tenth screenplay in a row read by the judge of an under-funded contest, working on deadline. What if his or her mind was weary after reading half a dozen bad screenplays in a row, and he or she simply failed to spot your brilliance? Judge fatigue does happen.

The numbers don't improve by submitting the same screenplay to more than one contest. If you enter ten contests, each with the same number of entrants, thus spending $400, then your chances of placing are the same one in a hundred because in ten contests, you're competing against ten times as many entrants.

One way to slightly improve your raw, numerical odds is to submit more than one very good screenplay to the same contest. Given the number of entries in the example cited, two screenplays means your numerical odds of placing would then be one in 50. Obviously, that is still very slim odds, but it's double what the odds are with one screenplay.

* * *

The Motion Picture Academy's Nicholl Fellowships are almost universally deemed to be the best contest to enter.

However, by some objective measures, this contest is not one of the best to enter. Here's why:

1. It offers low odds of winning, with five winners. It had 7,511 entrants in 2014. The entry number declined slightly to 6,915, in 2016. Five out of 7,511 is a .000667 chance of winning and five out of 6,195 is a .000723 change of winning – that is, not one percent, not even a tenth of one percent, but 6.67 and 7.23 per ten thousand.

2. It doesn't offer free feedback. It began offering feedback for a fee only in 2015.

3. It has the most money to invest in you. So if any contest could afford to give free feedback, the Nicholl Fellowships could. The Motion Picture Academy holds an endowment from the industry of $5,624,000 for the Nicholl Fellowships. Earnings on this endowment are used to augment Nicholl income from entry fees and other sources. In 2014, the earnings from this endowment which were available to spend were $243,800. In addition, the Nicholl Fellowships' entry fees are high; the late-entry fee was $85 the last time I checked. That is the highest late-entry fee I know of. Presumably, the Nicholl Fellowships have other sources of income as well, such as program advertising, sponsorships, and donations.

In short, it's the most financially endowed contest by far, and yet it is among those which offer no benefits to non-winning entrants.

In fairness to the Nicholl Fellowships competition, in at least one very important way, it is by far the best contest to enter. Its name alone opens more doors for winners than any other contest, should you be so skilled (and, given the numbers and the vagaries of the tastes of contest judges, lucky) to place high or win.

That is, the Nicholl Fellowships contest (along with, to a lesser extent, a few other screenplay contests which are seen as "prominent" by the industry) do more of your marketing for you than most "lesser" contests do - if you win or place.

If you depend on a contest placement to do your marketing for you, then you're making a serious mistake, in my opinion. You need to do your own marketing to take fullest advantage of contest wins and placements. And winning or placing is easier in so-called "lesser" screenplay contests.

Also, It Is <u>So</u> Easy To Lose A Contest

Most of us are not perfectionists. We tend to forgive our own mistakes, especially mistakes made in the course of a major, intense effort like that of writing a screenplay. It can be exhausting, writing such a long piece against a deadline, and it is quite human to tell oneself, "I've done my best; this is enough." For evidence of this, just go back and read chapter 4, on why writers submit imperfect work when they know it's imperfect.

However, the truth is that it's not your best. It's only your best within the energy and knowledge and amount of patience you had at the time, or within that deadline. If your "best at the time" has spelling or grammatical errors, or any other mistakes (such as failing to vividly define a sympathetic and very human protagonist and his/her quest and weaknesses in the first five pages, and the antagonist and his/her quest in the first 10), your odds in most contests dwindle to zero – <u>within your first 10 pages</u>.

Also, screenplay contests do not forgive language or structural imperfections or dull, derivative, seen-that-before stories, or just plain unremarkable stories, or weak openings.

It is no wonder that writers feel frustrated, given the fact that you work hard on your screenplays, and it is difficult to see one's own mistakes. It is a natural but small and bitter comfort to cast blame on the contest if you wrote to exhaustion, but your screenplays are riddled with the sort of mistakes the industry sees as an epidemic.

As to other complaints:

1. On The Quality of Screenplay Contest Judges/ Readers:

In my screenplay contests, I stopped publicly listing our first-round judges once I began offering feedback because our judges were being subjected to vicious emails by a few would-be writers who couldn't take losing. However, in fairness to you, the list of judges for the finals is a good factor to consider when you're trying to decide which contest to enter. A list of prominent finals judges means not only that if your screenplay makes it that far, it will be read by a successful industry pro, but also that the contest has prominent industry affiliations.

As to whether screenplay contest readers are good enough for the job, I can't speak authoritatively for contests other than the contests I ran. However, this complaint, like the complaint that readers for producers and agents are incompetent, seems more like sour grapes than substance. The judges for my contests were experienced screenplay readers who also worked for producers, agents, and studios. Blaming a judge for your screenplay's failure in a contest may be comforting to the ego, but otherwise, it's a waste of your time.

2. Winning a contest typically doesn't get your script sold without significant effort on your part.

This is usually true, although there are many exceptions (see below). Generally, the assumption that a contest win or placement leads directly (and more or less automatically, judging by the way these complaints are phrased) to a sale is a mistake.

Why is this so? Here are the two main shortcomings of contest wins/placements – in and of and by themselves – as a

186

screenwriter's marketing strategy:

The boost they provide is fleeting. A contest sends its winning scripts or their loglines to its list of industry contacts once, and publicizes them in an announcement and press release just once. That single, fleeting bit of contact and publicity is simply not real marketing, despite the best intentions of the contest. Contests also typically list their winners and high-placing writers on their websites, but this passive marketing, in and of itself, is weak. A producer has to go to the website and look for past winners to see that information.

That initial industry contact by the contest is a good start on marketing, but it is only a start. Real marketing of anything, including a screenplay, demands that you deliver your message about your product to all your potential customers more than once, over a period of time. That's Advertising and Marketing 101.

Contests are hit-and-miss with regard to who is contacted. Typically, a producer will affiliate with a contest because he/she is seeking a particular kind of screenplay for a single niche. Given all the niches and sub-niches, and the various formats (feature, one-hour TV series, half-hour TV series, short TV series, et cetera), the odds are slim that your winning screenplay will be a close match for the sort of script that the producers affiliated with that contest are seeking at that moment in time.

Exceptions...

A caveat: It is difficult to prove or confirm that a contest alone, with no self-marketing whatsoever by the writer, led directly to a deal or representation. However, a quick look at the "success stories" pages of a few of the more widely recognized contests makes it obvious that writers' successes in the contest below did lead, by one path or another, to breaking in:

Stage 32 The Happy Writers:
https://www.stage32.com/happy-writers/contests/2nd-

Annual-Stage-32-Happy-Writers-Feature-Script-Contest

Script Pipeline:
https://scriptpipeline.com/category/success-stories

The Page Awards: https://pageawards.com/success-stories/

TrackingB: "I entered my spec script EXTANT in the pilot contest because I'd heard so much about TrackingB and its reputation for helping writers reach the holy grail of representation. Never in my wildest dreams did I imagine that eight months later, I'd be in production, going straight to series on CBS." – Mickey Fisher, TrackingB contest finalist

Scriptapalooza:
http://www.scriptapalooza.com/winners/wherearetheynow.php

Final Draft Big Break:
http://store.finaldraft.com/big-break-contest.html
(Click on the "Success Stories" tab on the left side of the page.)

Austin Film Festival Screenplay Contest:
https://austinfilmfestival.com/festival-and-conference-aff/success-stories/ (Click on tabs for each year's screenwriting success stories at the bottom of that page)

Table Read My Screenplay Contest (International Screenwriters Association):
https://tablereadmyscreenplay.com/success/

The Screencraft.org website lists a number of success stories at: https://screencraft.org/success/
In addition, I received an email from Screencraft in June 2017 describing additional successes by writers not listed on that web page.

These are just a few examples. There are many more. If

you are considering entering a contest, it's worth your time to do a bit of research, starting with the contest website, on how the contest's winners have fared.

Keep in mind that none of these websites can give you any idea of how much additional marketing the successful screenwriter might have done on her or his own, using that credential of contest success.

One additional note: A couple of producers/production executives commented for this book that they don't care whether or how many "lesser" contests your screenplay has won or you've won. One screenwriter made a similar comment.

That's not generally true, and it's probably not even exactly what some of those industry individuals mean. What they probably really mean is that your pitch has to be a sterling pitch for the story itself, not start out with "This screenplay won the..." or emphasize contest placements and victories. Contest successes are the sort of detail you add toward the bottom of your one-page pitch letter. Trying to make contest victories the "sizzle" of your pitch or query is bad marketing.

However, producers are human. Most people respond positively to kudos, credentials, rankings, and ratings. Consider all the TV commercials and print ads you receive which tout a prize, rating or ranking a product received. Chevrolet, for example, has a very clever commercial which makes it sound almost as if its entire product line wins all the quality awards every year. That stuff has a positive psychological effect on how the potential customer views the product, regardless of what the customer might say. General Motors wouldn't be spending tens of millions of dollars on those nationwide TV commercials if its ad agency did not know that this is true.

I frankly hate those commercials, but nonetheless, they force me to think "Chevrolet" and "quality" at the same time. I can't help it. Neither can most people. The same is true of producers. Any mark of distinction, properly used, helps you and your work stand out from the crowd.

3. Feedback

In my view, receiving feedback is the #1 reason for entering screenplay contests. Here are my next three, more or less in this order, although this is arguable:

#2. Winning something, even a quarterfinals placement, in order to have credits for your writer resumé, your self-marketing efforts, and your self-esteem.

#3. The prize money.

#4. That brief window of industry contacts gained immediately and directly from the contest.

In my opinion, all contests should offer basic feedback to all entrants free of charge.

Why No Feedback?
Creating A Contest Feedback System Is So Easy, An English Lit Major Can Do It

As I mentioned above, I ran screenplay contests.

Using generic, cheap software tools, I created an online judging and feedback system for my screenplay contests. It cost nothing but some labor on my part, and I have zero formal training in computers, information technology, or website development. I used online business tools my company was already using: a $300/year Surveymonkey.com subscription, which we used for a variety of other purposes, and an email blast host. I used Microsoft Excel to sort the results.

So...

If I – a guy with an English lit and filmmaking degrees, who has never taken a computer or web development course of any kind – could set up a standardized judging system which provided a simple way to send feedback, why can't all other contests do the same?

There is no reason but the will to do so. In my opinion,

basic first-round feedback (scores on prime aspects of screenwriting and a brief judge comment) should be offered by every screenplay contest to every entrant.

The one stern warning I would give to screenplay contests: you have to train your judges not to make the sort of caustic comments which industry screenplay readers often write for their bosses' eyes about screenplays they don't like. Commentary must be stated constructively. I learned that the hard way.

4. Detailed Feedback Is Another Story Entirely

As for detailed feedback, one writer commented above that contests should offer deep analysis, even to the extent of citing problems in particular lines:

> All of them should offer feedback on your screenplay, so we know it was actually read, and that feedback should be specific, for example, on page 15, this happens when it should indicate it is CLEARLY the protagonist's choice, etc.

I don't mean to be unkind here, but analysis this detailed is not a practical idea within the fee structure of any current contest. In the industry, that level of customized, page-specific, in-depth script analysis goes for a median price of just over $300* from a professional script analyst. Even basic Hollywood coverage costs more than the typical contest entry fee.

So how is a contest going to offer $300 or more worth of script analysis for each contestant when entry fees range from a low of $20 in some cases to that $85 Nicholl late entry fee – and also pay all the other costs of a contest? Answer: It can't. This idea is just not workable. It would be a great idea if it were.

*To see the actual rates for the sort of in-depth analysis the aspiring writer above is seeking, please feel free to download my e-book on script consultants and analysts. It's a bit dated, so I offer it as a free download because you bought

this book. It is at this URL:
http://screenwritingcommunity.net/analysts/best.script.analy
sts.pdf

5. "More Contests Are Needed"

More of them? I disagree. I have a list of more than 500
screenplay contests worldwide, and that list isn't all of them. I
think fewer contests would be vastly better. In my view, many
of the so-called "lesser" contests, the smaller ones, ought to
merge with others, which would improve their budgets,
allowing them to offer more marketing help and better prizes.

6. That Screenwriter's Fear, Mentioned Above, of Plagiarism Or Idea Theft By Contests

Worrying about theft of your work from entering a
contest is self-defeating. It also exhibits a fundamental
ignorance of what you need to do to market a screenplay. A
producer is more likely than a contest to be the culprit if theft
of intellectual property occurs, and even that likelihood is very
low.

Before a producer, agent, or contest looks at your work,
you will be required to execute a waiver of liability for alleged
theft. If you don't, none of them will read it. Then, many
producers, agents, and their script readers share screenplays
they like with each other, without asking you for permission.
(As mentioned above, this is how and why the extremely
influential Blacklist was founded.) <u>This is to your benefit: it's
free marketing!</u>

So if you are unwilling to enter your screenplay in a
contest for fear of its theft, how on Earth are you going to show
your work to producers and/or agents, who will probably
circulate it all over the industry if it's good but not what they
want at the moment?

Recommendation: file a copyright registration for your
work, and then just quit worrying that "They might steal my
idea!" If you believe someone has stolen your work, consult a
good entertainment copyright attorney.

7. "I have been winner, finalist and on the second place for half a dozen times now and never got a call from anybody who would be interested in my work. "

First, congratulations for winning and placing well! Those are great accomplishments! Second, for reasons discussed above, it is unlikely that the marketing help you will get from a screenplay contest will be adequate by itself. As I've written more than once in this book, marketing yourself and your work is your job, it's fundamental to your success, and it is an ongoing process.

Don't wait for them to call. Contact them!

8. "New writers are generally up against older experienced writers who know the in's and out of writing for contest organizers."

Yes, experience is definitely an advantage when writing with the hope of winning a contest. It is even more so when trying to write screenplays producers might buy. From the context, the writer of this comment seems to believe that this is somehow unfair. I think not.

As I've mentioned above, in his last blog before he died, Blake Snyder, the author of the world's most popular screenwriting book, Save The Cat, wrote (citing another brilliant writer, Malcolm Gladwell), that becoming an expert at anything requires putting 10,000 hours into learning and doing. Please see this web page:

http://www.savethecat.com/todays-blog/best-of-blakes-blogs-blakes-last-blog

Similarly, UCLA Professor Richard Walter has said it takes 10 years to become a good screenwriter. Academy-Award Winner Frank Darabont has discussed the years of work he put in before becoming successful.

In screenwriting, as in any profession, it normally takes time, effort, study, practice, years of failure and near misses, and acceptance of emotionally wrenching feedback to make it. If you wanted to be a brain surgeon or design bridges or automotive brake systems or airplane engines, would it be unfair to expect you to put in the time and learn the trade? No. Screenwriting is also a high-level profession, not a hobby. Experience and learning curves count for a lot, as in any profession.

Young person, if you have the fortitude to keep at it, then once you have put in the time and effort, you will not want it to be any other way. Perseverance is one of life's greatest virtues.

9. Regarding "Don't make it clear the copyrights that are lost."

The comment is a bit cryptic, but I think the writer means that by entering a contest, the writer loses ownership of the copyrights. This is not true in the vast majority of contests. The only competition I know of in which this might be true to a degree is the Amazon Studios contest, in which the writer does agree to give up some rights.

In that contest, the writer also receives the benefit (or suffers the indignity and harm, depending on your point of view) of other writers being able to rewrite the work on the Amazon site. For these very reasons, I would never enter the Amazon Studios contest. It's not my thing. However, there are writers who have benefited greatly, and who have had their careers launched through Amazon Studios.

Always read the contest rules and FAQs before entering, just as you should for any deal you make with any vendor of anything.

10. "Directors don't have to compete to win a job directing a project, actors don't have to send in audition tapes to a competition in order to show their talent, why make writers go through this farce?"

On what planet, in which galaxy far, far away, do directors and actors not compete intensely for work? They certainly do in this one. Fiercely.

Actors have to show up for casting-calls, for example.

194

Your typical Los Angeles actor probably spends quite a bit more money on parking and parking tickets at Hollywood casting calls than you do entering contests. And then, there are the enervating hours in Los Angeles crosstown traffic, while you get to enter contests with a few clicks of the mouse. Also, they have to somehow pay for audition videos and stills to show to casting directors, producers and agents, with no guarantee of being noticed.

Aspiring directors have it even worse. They have to create reels of their work, which typically involves someone spending a great deal more money producing a film or video than you spend entering contests. And then, they have to hope someone is willing to take the time to view that video and overlook the low-budget production values. Many directors take the route I took when I wanted to be a writer-director: three to four years of film school, and competing with every other student to be the director on the student productions with sufficient production value to show to the industry.

In other words, the competitions are different. However, the competition actors and directors face is at least as tough as the competition faced by aspiring screenwriters.

Also, you do not have to submit to contests in order to market your work. Contest feedback is a benefit, and a contest win or placement is a useful credential, but submitting to a contest is purely voluntary.

11. "Not clear how much credibility producers put on certain contests."

This is a bit repetitive, but I think it's important enough to repeat:

Judging from producers' responses to the industry survey for this book (and based on many years of keeping careful tabs on what people respond to in a marketing sales pitch), I'm fairly sure that the following is true:

If asked, most producers would say they give credibility to only a few "top" contests. However, if a great query letter and great logline arrived, and if the script were the sort that producer were seeking at that time, then the mention, toward the bottom of the query, that the script had placed well in a couple of "lesser" contests would help to pique that producer's interest. Every relevant credential, in its proper place and proportion, is better than no credential at all.

In such a case, the producer would be more likely to ask to read the screenplay, and the contest placement would be a positive factor in placing it ahead of a script with no contest credits.

12. "larger cash prizes through sponsors" … "or…have it produced…"

I've run 11 screenplay contests. Please tell me where to find those sponsors for the large cash prizes. I spent a lot of time hunting for sponsors. People who want to endow a screenplay contest are few and far between.

As for producing the winning script…

If it's a short, and the script doesn't call for any significant production costs, sure. However, for a feature, a "micro" budget is about $250,000. Certainly, a feature could be produced for less, maybe for as little as $100,000 if you don't mind it looking inexpensive, if the script allows for free locations far from Los Angeles, if it can be shot without a lot of expensive lighting, if it uses unknown actors who work for deferred pay and who pay for their own room and board far from Los Angeles, if there are no special effects, if you use a cheap camera, and if you have a small, non-union crew who also work for deferred pay and pay their own room and board.

However, take that apocryphal contest with 2,000 entries x $40 entry fee discussed above, with $80,000 in total sales, as an example. It has contest expenses to pay (see below). Where does that $250,000, or even $100,000, to produce a feature, come from?

In short, screenplay contests do not make enough money to support that sort of prize. Even the Nicholl Fellowships competition, if it were to try to offer an ultra-low-budget feature as a prize, would have to eliminate its five $35,000 screenwriting fellowships in favor of one micro-budget production.

Some of these comments reflect the inability of aspiring screenwriters, who have never run businesses or produced movies, to visualize what it costs to run a screenplay contest, and where the money goes. That is why I'm ending this chapter with the spreadsheet below.

Choose to disbelieve it if you wish, but again, this is a composite set of facts based on four years of actual income and expenses from a real screenplay contest:

Composite 4-Year Average Budget
Of An Actual Screenplay Competition

Income and Expense Items	Unit Price	Number	Subtotal
Income Items			
Entry Fees:			
Entries: Early, $45 Each	$45	291	$13,095
Entries: On Time, $50 Each	$50	345	$17,250
Entries: "Midnight Oil," $55 Each	$55	235	$12,925
Entries: After Extension, $60 Each	$60	235	$14,100
Entries: WithoutABox, $37 Each Net	$36	247	$8,892
Number of feature entries:		1353	
Entries – Teleplay contest	$30	100	$3,000
Subtotal, Entries			**$69,262**
Sponsors and Advertisers – Estimate			
Cash sponsorships	$400	1	$400
Advertisers	$400	2	$800
Subtotal, Sponsors and Advertisers			**$1,200**

Total Revenue $70,462

Expense Items

Bad check losses	$45	30	$1,350
Credit card processing fees	3%		$1,870

Advertising and Promotion			
Artwork for magazine ads	$400	1	$400
Magazine Ads (see note)	$1,500	2	$3,000
Artwork for web site ad images	$100	4	$400
Labor -write/manage e-mail blasts	$100	6	$600
Withoutabox email blast	$450	1	$450
Email blast advertising (see note)	$1,000	6	$6,000
Third-party email, site ads:			
Moviebytes	$425	3	$1,275
Screenplaycontests.com	$300	2	$600
Done Deal Pro	$200	3	$600
ScreenwritersUtopia	$200	2	$400
Subtotal, advertising costs			**$13,725**

Contest staff (other than judges)

Web site contractors			$500
Contest entry system annual update			$600
Update 350-producer mailing list	$20	20	$400
Customer service (phone, emails)	$15	100	$1,500
Contest manager hours	$20	220	$4,400
Contest Manager Incentive Pay			$2,024
Labor: distributing scripts to judges	$1	1453	$727

Subtotal, staff expense $10,151

Out-Of-Pocket Office Expenses

Supplies, postage, incidentals			$150
Distribution of winning synopses to 350 producers and agents:			
Postage	$1.13	350	$396
Labor	$15.00	30	$450
Subtotal, Out-Of-Pocket Expenses			**$996**

Overhead Expense

AAA Contest overhead is estimated to be 3% of total company budget (see note).	$6,204	1	**$6,204**

Script Judging

Regular Entries	$10	1353	$13,530
Feature script second-round judging	$15	88	$1,319
Teleplays	$9	100	$900
Teleplay second-round judging	$12	10	$120
Subtotal, script judging			**$15,869**

Prizes
1. Cash prizes and prize expenditures

Grand Prize	$5,000	1	$5,000
Special Jury Prize	$3,000	1	$3,000
Runnersup	$1,000	2	$2,000
Teleplay Prizes	$500	2	$1,000
Publicity for winners	$500	1	$500
Subtotal, prize costs			**$11,500**

2. Non-monetary prizes (see note)

Gold Pass To Screenwriting Expo	$350	1	$350
Basic passes to Screenwriting Expo	$125	12	$1,500
Creative Screenwriting subscriptions	$24	13	$312
Subtotal, in-kind prizes provided by us:			**$2,162**

Average Out-Of-Pocket Expense	**$63,826**

Average Net Profit	**$6,636**

Notes On The Composite Budget Above

Providing actual expenses for a screenwriting contest necessarily involves some assumptions and definitions. For example, if the organization running the contest offers other services (as we did), then the costs for staffing and office overhead* have to be allocated between the contest(s) and these other services.

*What is "overhead"? For those with no business experience, it is expenses which are not associated with a particular product line or service, such as rent, utilities, supplies, furniture and equipment, computers, Internet access, bookkeeping, accounting, taxes other than sales taxes, executive and receptionist, staffing phones during business hours, bookkeeping and accounting pay, and other expenses incurred by the entire organization.

In the composite budget above, I attributed a conservative 3% of our total office overhead to that contest. Five to eight percent would have been more accurate, but I didn't want to be accused of inflating contest expenses.

Moreover, for a contest organization which has no other sources of income than the contest itself, then 100% of office overhead and staffing would have to be paid from contest income. Whether there is one product line or there are fifty product lines, a business operation needs a chief executive, a customer service staff, a furnished office, utilities, bookkeeping and accounting, and positive cash flow each month or extra money in the bank.

Therefore, the overhead for a contest which has no other services would be a smaller total than ours, but the contest would be paying all of it, so it would be a bigger part of the budget.

Most contests use either Withoutabox or Film Freeway, or both, for two purposes: promotion/marketing and to have a contest entry system, allowing scripts to be digitally uploaded. Film Freeway was not around when these contests were run. Using Withoutabox incurred three sets of significant costs:

1. Contests had to offer a lower entry fee to those who entered through its portal.

2. Withoutabox also takes a percentage of those lower

entry fees off the top.

3. Withoutabox also charges to send advertising to writers.

One could debate the legitimacy of some of our expenses, such as the non-monetary prizes we offered, averaging $2,612 per year. Some might argue that these weren't actually costs because they were services we already provided. However, they were indeed real costs because

(a) we had to spend money to produce them and

(b) it is extremely likely that the recipients would have purchased these services if they hadn't been offered as prizes.

So offering them as prizes cost us these amounts in sales.

Similarly, you might argue that since we owned Creative Screenwriting Magazine and our email blast list, the $9,000 in expense allocated to advertising in the magazine and via email blasts wasn't "real." To a degree, this was true for our contest budget, due to our unique position. It certainly cost us less to advertise than it would have cost any of the hundreds of other contests, which didn't have their own magazine and 120,000-person email blast list as advertising media.

But again, these resources cost money, too. Leaving them out of the budget would create a false picture of a typical contest's true operating costs. If we hadn't had these advertising outlets, we would have spent more than $9,000 on third-party advertising, as other contests must do. A contest must advertise, or contest entry revenues would be much lower.

This composite of budgets omits a few contest-specific expenses (plaques, costs of a reception and dinner for winners, and a few others) because I couldn't find those figures. So, rather than guess, I left those expenses out. However, they're real.

As you can see from the numbers, the average annual revenues from entry fees and all other sources for the screenplay contest over four years was slightly less than

$70,000. Annual expenses averaged $63,826. Net profit averaged $6,636. Also, even with our advertising outreach and cash prizes, which were both more than the average contest could afford then or can afford now, the number of entries in this contest never reached that theoretical 2,000 the complaining writer assumed.

Even the net profit figure is misleading. In two years, when total entries and entry fees were low, the contest lost money.

Hopefully, this composite budget will inform some writers as to where your contest entry fees go. The notion that a contest can make $70,000 in profit on $80,000 in entry fees is quite far from reality.

13: Be That One In A Hundred At Pitch Events

The odds of selling your screenplay at a pitch event are long, but they're better than with most other approaches. Also, pitch events offer additional opportunities. Overall, they're among the best approaches to getting your screenplay read.

Here are some reasons the odds are not great, and ways to improve them.

1. "Blockbuster Or Bust" Disease

When I ran the Screenwriting Expo, our pitch event was a ticket system. That is, unlike the Great American Pitch Fest (now called Scriptfest.com), at our pitch event you needed a ticket to pitch a particular producer, agent, or studio.

There are huge technical difficulties in selling tickets to individual pitches. However, our system did have one advantage: it allowed me to see how many tickets were sold for each pitch recipient (producer or agent). I watched those sales carefully.

And this much was obvious: writers practically fought each other for tickets to pitch to studio-owned production companies and a few top independent production companies.

Meanwhile, tickets to pitch to less-known production companies, which were more seriously looking for a script in their day at the pitch event, went begging.

I highlighted in our advertising and promotional materials for our pitch event that writers should pitch the smaller companies because there were far greater chances of selling a script. I argued that case again and again.

To little avail. A great many pitch event attendees suffered from "Blockbuster or Bust" disease. That's a failing strategy. To build a screenwriting career, think of the "bigs" as a long shot, and those smaller independent producers as your real opportunities.

2. Your Screenplay Isn't The Story They Want At This Moment. So Now, What?

Even when you narrow your target producers to those who work in the genre you're pitching, you have no way of knowing what that producer is seeking that day. He or she might not even know.

Or he/she might be seeking something too specific: a buddy story in outer space with five oddball characters from various planets, one of whom is keen on late '60s-early '70s pop, another a beautiful green female, one's a wisecracking furry little animal, and another seems to be a tree ... But you're hawking a buddy space opera in which the huge sidekick looks and sounds a lot like a big ol' Wookie, and you're emotionally invested in the dialogue you've written in the Thykarann language for the big hairy creature.

Well, there goes that meeting of the minds.

This is what a pitch event is like. Your screenplay is one item on a menu of a thousand scripts being presented to a hundred or two hundred very finicky producers, agents, and maybe studio people who are usually looking for something else, if they know what they want at all.

In other words, the chance that you are going to sell something at a pitch event is low. That is no one's fault.

However, at least you and they are meeting face to face, which is otherwise difficult to achieve. So here are two ways to be prepared to make the best of a pitch event:

First, come with more than one good script to pitch. Have more than one feature written, and have a TV show or two written. Pitch only one per pitch, but be ready to pitch the others to the right producers.

Second, pitch with the idea that it is equally (or more) important to impress the customer with yourself: your manners, your creative intelligence, your understanding of the industry, your deference to their judgment, and your willingness to take notes and do rewrites.

Here are a couple more pitch event tips:

One: If you have a five-minute window, limit your pitch to three minutes. Then, at the right moment – whether the producer is interested or not – ask for the producer's advice on what to change. The reason to ask is twofold: first, you might hear a really good idea, and second, and far more important, asking that question implies that you are one of those true professionals who accepts Notes and critiques.

Two: Always say "thank you" on the spot, and then write a handwritten thank-you note on small creme-colored thank-you stationery to every producer or agent you've sat across from. Why?

"The world runs on thank-yous."

I wrote this in chapter 1, and I'm repeating it because it is so important, and so universally ignored. Again, the man who said those words raised almost $100 million for a soup kitchen, which now offers a lot more services to the neediest of the needy. People who gave money initially ended up coming back and giving more. The secret of "thank-you" notes is that you'll be remembered as that one aspiring screenwriter in a thousand who writes them.

3. Again, Sell Yourself, Not Only The Script

If you think your only purpose in being there is that script you're pitching, you are missing the Big Picture. The Big Picture is that you are there to persuade that producer or agent to invest in you, whether through that script or something else. That script is both its own product and a demo – a way of describing what is inside you that is worth investing in.

How do you sell yourself? Do I mean that you're supposed to dedicate part of your pitch time to talking about how great you are? No. "You" will shine through, for better or worse, in how you pitch the script.

4. You're Pitching Features; They're Buying TV Shows

There are many more TV series work being sold these days than big-budget features. So what are you pitching? You just went to a pitch event with that one big-budget feature script you've slaved over. But no one is interested.

Swim with the tide, not against it.

This is doubly so when pitching agents. They make more money off clients who work regularly for TV.

5. Take Pitching Classes

Most pitch events offer classes on site on how to pitch. However, in my view, your best chances of learning how to pitch are to take classes or tutorials in advance and also take on-site pitch classes. Then, practice your pitch in front of others and in front of a mirror before you give it.

Some of the top screenwriting teachers offer classes and tutorials on how to pitch, many of which you can take from a distance. Michael Hauge's class on the two-minute pitch is an example:

Beginning the Two-minute pitch (free on Youtube):

https://www.youtube.com/watch?v=BGuFfuFuaCY

His DVD: The Two-Minute Pitch:
http://www.storymastery.com/shop/dvds/dvd-mastering-2-minute-pitch/

He also has an excellent article at the Writers Store website, "Mastering the Three-Minute Pitch," at:

https://www.writersstore.com/secrets-of-the-3-minute-pitch/

NOTE: He is not the only teacher who offers classes on pitching, of course, and there are many other resources available online to help you learn to pitch. Google "how to pitch a screenplay to a producer" or "how to pitch a script to a producer" for a long list of links.

6. The Caped Pitch Crusaders...

I had heard before I went to my first pitch event that

there are people who pitch in costumes. I didn't believe it. I didn't think anyone would be that naive. Pitching is not a cosplay convention or Comic-Con. The idea is to convince the producer that you're that calm, skilled, brilliant writer with an abundant supply of creative ideas and on-the-money (but not on-the-nose) dialogue swirling around in your head. You're not the actor. And you had definitely better not be the character.

But then, at my first Expo, there he was: That Guy. The one heading into the pitch event wearing a black cape billowing in the air, like Bela Lugosi floating into the room in the 1931 "Dracula."

Oh, dear. Poor fellow. Don't do that.

(Exception: A produced writer I know did sell a show to Disney in a pitch in which he briefly did some character roles, male and female, in their voices. The pitch worked. I'm sure that approach has worked elsewhere, but it has to be done well, and only in limited moments during a pitch.)

Another memorable pitch event attendee, for the wrong reasons, was a woman with wild hair and a tangle of news clippings and notes hanging out of her overstuffed brief bag. She would stand at the exit door of our pitch event, and as the next group came in from the "enter" side to pitch, she'd wait until everyone was seated, then rush an empty seat across from a producer. It didn't seem to matter which producer, or which genre that producer wanted.

It's unkind to say, but she seemed more like a character in a screenplay than a writer. Don't be her at a pitch event. Act as if you're rational.

List Of In-Person And Online Pitch Events

Here's a list of pitch events I found in the U.S. as of 9/3/2017:

1. In-Person Pitch Events

207

Great American Pitchfest/Scriptfest:
http://scriptfest.com/home/

Austin Film Festival Pitch Day:
https://austinfilmfestival.com/event/pitch-day/

Ken Rotcop's Pitchmart:
http://www.pitchmart.com/

Fade In Online Hollywood Pitch Festival:
https://fadeinonline.com/hollywood-pitch-festival

2. Online Pitch Events

Virtual Pitch Fest:
https://virtualpitchfest.com/

Fade In Online:
https://fadeinonline.com/hollywood-pitch-festival-online

There may be others.

14: The Path To Success

How To Maximize Your Chances Of A Sale And A Career, Briefly Summarized

The Script

1. Your grammar and spelling must be perfect, or nearly so. Never send out a screenplay which is anything less.

2. The basic formatting has to be right. Not only should you get it right, but don't be avant-garde. Format for the most conservative reader.

3. Stick to three-act structure. Some producers will forgive structure problems if the characters and dialogue are great. But how do you know they're going to be the ones who read your script? You don't.

4. Your story must be new, fresh, and original, not imitative, a knockoff, a copycat, derivative, a rehash, or a superficial story populated with shallow characters.

5. It should fit a recognizable genre, niche, or emerging social trend, preferably one which is currently more in vogue than other genres and niches.

6. Something about it has to be <u>great</u>. Usually, that means you need a great protagonist with clear flaws and goals, opposed by an equally great antagonist, and great dialogue.

7. Ignore the top of the movie charts. For screenplay models, look down the charts to the independently produced movies made and released, and at the growing number of original TV series being produced these days.

8. Think of your spec screenplays as calling-cards. There is more money to be made in rewrites of already-purchased screenplays and writing for TV than in selling spec scripts.

Your Behavior

1. Always exhibit perfect manners. Say "thank you." Write "thank you" notes.

2. Treat everyone, especially support staff, at every industry-related organization as if they were Steven Spielberg himself.

3. Never, ever, ever curse at or flame anyone in the business – not in person, not by email, not on the phone, not even "anonymously" on social media or a chat board.

4. Drop the attitude. Do you believe "My script and I are as important as the stars," or some other iteration of self-importance? Stuff it. That will be true when you write the next "Juno" or "Slumdog Millionaire," "Jaws," or "Gone With The Wind"and it proves itself in the marketplace of ticket sales or eyes glued to the TV screen. Until then, it's not true.

5. You have to do your own marketing of your work or pay for marketing and manage it. Marketing is difficult to learn. It is difficult to do well. Unless you get lucky very quickly, it is more time-consuming than writing a script. And it costs money. The only good thing to say about marketing is that it is how you get a sale.

That's this book in a nutshell.

Well, actually, one more thing...

Never Blame Others.
Never Make Excuses
For Your Lack Of Success

The thought above came to me while reading the comments in Chapter 11 by aspiring screenwriters who complain that "the industry" or "producers" want "fluffy things," that producers don't understand the craft, that they are obsessed with immediately sellable "IPs," that all they do is recycle previous hits, that all they're interested in is franchises, that they pretend they're indie-friendly, that they are "too commercial," or that there's a lot of "rehashed garbage out there."

Yes, each of these complaints is true of some produced content. It's also true that in many cases, the biggest marketing budgets go to some of those sorts of movies.

However, that is not true of the industry as a whole. Simply not so. You are deluding and sabotaging yourself if you believe it is.

Also, it's not called the "entertainment foundation," the "entertainment charity," or the "entertainment government agency for the welfare of aspiring writers." It's called the entertainment <u>business</u>. Like other businesses, it's run by people who put up the investment money with the expectation of making a profit, not the expectation of losing money on great works of cinematic art (which happen anyway every year, along with all the profitable content you might think of as "rehashed garbage").

This "Don't blame others" thought came back again while I was rewriting the chapter on writers' complaints about screenplay contests. Contests are easy to blame because upwards of 95% of entrants to a contest spend money and then are rejected. I can easily understand your frustration and desire to blame contests. I briefly blamed them when I didn't win.

However, the evidence abounds that writers win contests and then break into the industry. Yes, some contests are mediocre. A very, very few are outright scams. But by and large, screenplay contests are a stepping stone toward a career if you know how to use them in your marketing. Blaming contests for your lack of success only hurts the blamer.

So why tell yourself such self-defeating lies? The comfort you receive is fleeting, and the sense of defeat remains. To join the small percentage who succeed, keep up your morale, make yourself a better screenwriter, and equally important, be a better marketer of your work.

I hope this book helps in a small way.

Bill Donovan
BeThatOneInAHundred.com

15: Sources Of The Information In This Book

The bulk of the information in this book came from surveys of industry professionals and interviews with producers.   Other information is as cited.

In the surveys, of 412 survey responses, 147 identified themselves as industry professionals. Of these 147 industry respondents...

- 65 are producers
- 6 are agents
- 22 are script readers for agents, producers, or studios
- 51 are screenplay consultants/analysts and screenwriting teachers
- 27 are contest executives and judges
- 20+ are produced screenwriters who have read other screenwriters' work.

The numbers above and below add up to more than the number of respondents because some respondents have more than one role in the industry.

After studying the industry survey results, the author sent a survey to aspiring screenwriters seeking their perspectives on the comments by the industry. The survey was closed after 129 responses. Of those 129:

- 91 are screenwriters who say they have not yet sold or optioned a script yet
- 15 have had screenplays of theirs produced
- 5 more have sold at least one screenplay, but have not had one produced
- 17 have had work optioned, but have not sold a screenplay yet
- 5 said they are not screenwriters at all.

Also, among the responding writers:

- 91 say they hold no other job or position in the industry
- 5 are readers for producers, agents, or studios
- 22 are producers as well as writers
- One of the produced writers who responded is also an agent

- 9 are screenwriting teachers
- 12 are screenplay consultants or analysts
- 4 are screenplay contest judges
- None are in screenplay contest executive management.
- 34 hold other industry positions, including: Actors, an actor/director, aspiring filmmaker, previously subtitle editor, script reader, film accountant, assistant director and unit production manager, associate and executive producer of several shorts, directors, documentary filmmaker, editors, entertainment law document clerk/records mgr., film extra, a writer who had musicals for stage produced, locations manager, media editor, mentors of screenwriters, multiple contest winner who runs a screenwriting group in his/her city, multiple writing, directing, director of photography and production design credits in industrial and event videos along with one entertainment production designer credit and several art department credits, producer, director, and editor, production assistant, script supervisor and caterer, production coordinator, electrician, reader, SAG-AFTRA member/actor, screenwriter with multiple works based upon his or her original novels, script supervisor; production assistant, set and costume designer, sound editor, WGA-w representative.

Some of the information in this book comes from the author's personal experience, first as an aspiring screenwriter quite a few years ago, and then from his more recent experience as the owner of the Creative Screenwriting enterprise. In that position, he was, among other roles, the executive in charge of screenplay contests and pitch events, a screenplay judge in his company's screenplay contests, the chief executive and editor of Creative Screenwriting Magazine and the executive producer of the Screenwriting Expo and its Golden Pitch Event.

About The Author

Over several years as the owner and chief executive of Creative Screenwriting Magazine, the Screenwriting Expo, their screenplay contests, and their educational DVDs for screenwriters, Bill Donovan had contacts with thousands of aspiring screenwriters, more than two dozen Oscar winners and screenwriters of Hollywood blockbusters, and more than a hundred produced screenwriters in all.

He was once an aspiring screenwriter himself. While earning a master's degree in film production and screenwriting at the University of Southern California, he won three student screenwriting awards in three tries and had agents for his screenplays twice; none of his screenwriting work was ever sold.

This is his fourth book for screenwriters. The other three are outdated and no longer for sale.

His credentials and qualifications as a researcher include years of working as a reporter and editor for daily newspapers, the Associated Press, and multiple business-to-business news publications. He won or shared five national business journalism awards during his years of working for business publications.

Since 2012, at Screenwritingcommunity.net, he has offered his screenwriting books as well as proofreading and story comments to screenwriters and advertising opportunities to people and businesses selling services and products to screenwriters.

He can be reached by email at:
bill@BeThatOneInAHundred.com
or by surface mail at PO Box 6735, Big Bear Lake CA 92315.

42215077R00136

Made in the USA
Columbia, SC
16 December 2018